Coventry:
A Century of News

ALTON DOUGLAS

DENNIS MOORE

ADDITIONAL RESEARCH BY

JO DOUGLAS

© 1991 Alton Douglas, Dennis Moore, Jo Douglas
ISBN 0 902464 36 1

Published by Coventry Newspapers Ltd., Corporation Street, Coventry CV1 1FP.
Printed by Page Bros, Mile Cross Lane, Norwich, Norfolk, NR6 6SA

Greyfriars Lane, near to the corner with Cow Lane and Union Street, 1953

Dear Reader,

One hundred years of publishing news and comment on Coventry and Warwickshire. February 9th 1991 marks that historic landmark for the Coventry Evening Telegraph.

In the first issue the editor wrote: 'On public questions we shall be entirely independent, owning allegiance to no sect and to no community, but exercising the fullest freedom in dealing with matters which may come under our notice. To be a newspaper first and last and always is the purpose we shall seek to accomplish'. 100 years later that still applies and much of the success of the newspaper can be attributed to such a philosophy, in particular keeping free of political affiliations.

The City of Coventry changed so much in the period. Motors, aircraft, machine-tools came and with them workers and their families from the four corners of the British Isles and from overseas. The city grew in size in housing and shopping until a large part of it was devastated in the Second World War. The Blitz and its effects have been chronicled elsewhere but it led to a complete re-generation, of the city centre in particular. Coventry's expansion continued until the 1980s which unfortunately saw massive reductions of output and staff in companies involved in the engineering industries.

An appreciation of the impact of those losses on the future of the city brought about a decision on a re-direction and re-birth of commerce and industry in new technology industries with Science Parks, Business Parks, and a significant re-development in the city centre. Optimism for the future is now very apparent.

In all this time the Coventry Evening Telegraph - it was the Midland Daily Telegraph until November 17th 1941 - recorded and reflected what was happening at the time. The newspaper itself did not stand still. In 1900 it was the first provincial newspaper to use motor vehicles for delivery. It kept up to date over the years with changing technology and in 1965 it pioneered colour printing. Hot metal print was replaced by photocomposition and now just at the time of its 100th birthday we shall see a new offset press producing colour each day.

The Coventry Evening Telegraph is proud of its achievements over the 100 years and is pleased to publish a pictorial record of the city and a flavour of the newspapers we have produced to record events and happenings. We hope you get great pleasure from reading this book - the elderly from remembering the past and the young in appreciating the history of this great City of Coventry.

Chairman
Coventry Newspapers Limited

February 1991

Coventry Evening Telegraph

the City's newspaper

"Read all about it! Latest score — 100 (not out)" — the cry of the street-corner newsvendor, so beloved of film-makers, still has a nostalgic ring even in these modern times.

No doubt the newsboys of February 9, 1891, could not have known just what an impact a brand-new broadsheet (just four pages, folded once and titled "The Midland Daily Telegraph"), would soon have on its readers.

When local printer William I. Iliffe founded the newspaper, Coventry's population was barely 52,000, well under the limit of 100,000, a figure below which no newspaper in any city of that size could hope to flourish. But flourish it did.

Let us travel along an imaginary lane in the city, a lane with Victorian back-to-back houses at one end, Edwardian villas in the middle and modern detached residences at the other end.

The house numbers are high ones, for it is a long lane. No. 1891 is privileged to have the very first edition of "The Midland Daily Telegraph" delivered to its door. Further along, there is a welcome home for a worker at the new Daimler Motor Co. factory, a gleam in his eye as he opens his first pay-packet.

The loyal folk at No. 1901 are saddened to read in their local newspaper of the death of Queen Victoria but later cheer to celebrate the crowning of the new King Edward VII. A khaki-coloured edition of "The Midland Daily Telegraph" is delivered to 1902, welcoming back troops who had volunteered for the Boer War.

Judging by the number of bikes propped against fences all along the lane, cycling seems popular with residents who own locally-made bicycles; and is not the Premier Cycle Co. of Coventry claiming to be the biggest of its kind in the world? Our lane boasts a new motor car at No. 1904, built in Coventry by the Rover Cycle Co. (later the Rover Co.).

The family at No 1910 read that Edward VII has died and that King George V has succeeded him. Poppies bloom in the front gardens of Nos. 1914 to 1918 (as well as in the flower-beds at Nos. 1939 to 1945). Sad to read that an enemy air-raid has destroyed properties at No. 1940 and its near neighbours; happily they are restored in modern style and receive the newly-titled "Coventry Evening Telegraph" through their letterboxes on November 17, 1941.

Union Flags flutter in royal celebration at No. 1953 and the new-born daughter there is christened Elizabeth. Lord Iliffe (son of the founder) lays the foundation stone of the new Corporation Street building to house the growing "Coventry Evening Telegraph" and the man of the house at No. 1957 reads about it in the "Evening Telegraph"

When the residents at No. 1971, with their neighbours, realise that the edition in their hands is numbered 25,000, they are justifiably proud of the achievements of their favourite local newspaper.

The people living in this lane of ours have witnessed a long history of local newspaper success and, furthermore, the end house, No. 1991, seems ready to welcome builders to erect more homes next to it and further along the lane. The name of this lane? Why — "Memory Lane" of course!

"The Coventry Evening Telegraph" (and its predecessor "The Midland Daily Telegraph") has never missed producing an edition in all of its 100 years of publishing. Even on November 15, 1940, after that devastating air-raid, the paper was still printed and sold outside the city, although no copies were sold within.

Here's to the "Coventry Evening Telegraph" and the next century of news.

CAMERA PRINCIPIS

Midland Daily Telegraph.

NO. 1. VOL. I.   HEAD OFFICE: 16, HERTFORD ST., COVENTRY.   MONDAY, FEBRUARY 9, 1891.   REGISTERED FOR TRANSMISSION AS A NEWSPAPER FOR THE UNITED KINGDOM AND ABROAD.   ONE HALFPENNY.

5

The Coventry Football Club team, April 8, 1891

Pennington's tandem motor cycle on the Butts track, 1892

A Rudge five-seater cycle at Monks Kirby, 1897

E. J. Pennington and his friends travel on the "New Pennington Autocar," 1897

QUEEN VICTORIA'S DIAMOND JUBILEE

June 25, 1897.

"TUESDAY morning opened dull, but there was no rain, and the forecast was favourable. There was an early ringing of church bells, and the National Anthem was played by bands on Grey Friars Green. The longed-for day had come, and by 10 o'clock it was evident that there was to be Queen's weather for Queen's Day. Nobody went to work except journalists and domestics, yet most citizens laboured hard. The shops and factories were all closed.

The streets were sought directly after breakfast and all ways seemed to lead to Pool Meadow, where the Sunday school children were massing. Excursion trains came in bringing their living freights from two-score and more places. The city looked splendid under a genial sky, and with people in holiday attire, and in holiday mood.

The streets and lanes, and even the courts, too, were decked in brightest colours. National flags and banners waved in the breeze and bunting covered the fronts of the houses.

NEVER BEFORE

The unanimous verdict of the immense number of persons who witnessed the Sunday scholars' demonstration of a similar character had not been seen in Coventry. Nearly the whole of the 14,000 scholars carried red, white or blue flags, Union Jacks or Japanese umbrellas, and the effect viewed from the platform erected near the School of Art was charming.

A pageant in which Lady Godiva rode was also staged, and everyone who took part wore medieval costume, including "The Lady."

No doubt the city thoroughfares were hot, with crowds moving about, but the people were good tempered, and the 22nd June, in the 60th year of the Queen's reign was one never to be forgotten.

First Coventry-to-Birmingham run, leaving Greyfriars Green, 1897

8

The Duchess of Albany, in town to open the bazaar at St Thomas's, poses with various dignitaries, including the Mayor, Dr Webb Fowler, 1898

Children's party in Queens Road Baptist Church, c.1900

Flooding in Godiva Street, early Monday morning, December 31, 1900

— May 25, 1900.

THE news of the relief of Mafeking, which had been so anxiously and sorrowfully awaited, was received in Coventry on Friday night.

During the day, the city had been in an extraordinarily quiet state, probably as a reaction from the excitement of the previous day in consequence of the rumoured relief of the long-besieged town. At half-past nine at night Broadgate and the streets in the centre of the city were almost deserted; their quietude being all the more marked in contrast with the proceedings 24 hours before.

Death of Queen Victoria in 1901

January 25, 1901.

HER MAJESTY, Queen Victoria, passed peacefully away at Osborne, Isle of Wight, at half past six, on Thursday evening. Words are too feeble to express the depth of grief into which we, as Nation and an Empire, are plunged. The Queen's long and glorious reign covered almost the allotted span of human life.

Today the faithful members of her household, the devoted tenants, and the labourers on the estate filed past her dead body, took their final view of her, and paid their last respects. Every one of Her Majesty's employees were invited to attend, from the steward of the estate to the humblest farm servant, came and none failed.

His Majesty, King Edward VII, leaving the deathbed of his revered parent, arrived on Wednesday in the capital, to take up the burden of sovereignty

Bond's Hospital, c.1901

Homecoming of the Coventry Volunteer Service Company from the Boer War, Coventry Station, April 30, 1901

11

12

13

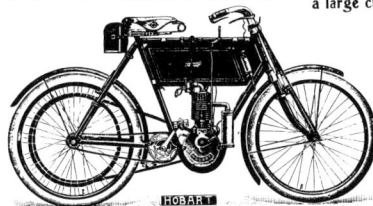

14

Naul's Mill Park, c.1905

1906

THE History of the Motor Trade in Coventry is practically that of the Daimler Company, for Coventry is the Home of the Motor Trade, and Automobilists of all Countries are attracted to that industrious centre. The Motor Trade in Coventry is about ten years old, the first Car having been produced there by the Daimler Company in 1896. The Daimler Company was one of a group of Companies created by a promoter who, however much his desire for immediate gain may have biassed its commercial stability, had, nevertheless, a remarkable eye to the future.

The foundation stone of the Empire, Hertford Street

31st Aug 1906

WHEATLEY STREET BOYS' SCHOOL.

Quarterly Report of *Arthur Wilson*

SUBJECTS.	POSITION.
READING	First
WRITING	2
COMPOSITION AND DICTATION	First—22
ARITHMETIC	2
MENTAL ARITHMETIC	2
GRAMMAR	2
RECITATION	3
HISTORY	First
GEOGRAPHY	5
DRAWING	2
PHYSIOLOGY	2
ELECTRICITY	2
ATTENDANCE	&c.
PUNCTUALITY	V. Good
HOME WORK	&c.
GENERAL INTELLIGENCE	&c.
CONDUCT	Good
ALGEBRA	Good

No. in the Class.

32

General Position in Class.

First

REMARKS: Arthur now occupies the front position of first boy in the school. I am very pleased with his work.

J. Potter   *Class Master.*

W. M. Darrell   *Head Master.*

Godiva procession, 1907

*An overturned tram at Lower
Ford Street corner, 1907*

Humber's Stoke car factory, 1908

GIRLS had to sneak away from their outraged parents to go to Gosford Gym Club in 1908.

They wore ankle-length skirts and voluminous blouses to contradict any accusation of immodesty.

And although men and women did physical exercises in the same building . . . it was never at the same time.

Yet in the 1900's the founder at Gosford Street Baptist Church, Mrs. Nobel and Mr. Innocent, were labelled avant garde.

Humber, 1909

Coventry Esperanto Club, c.1910

Coventry Rambling Club, c.1910

17

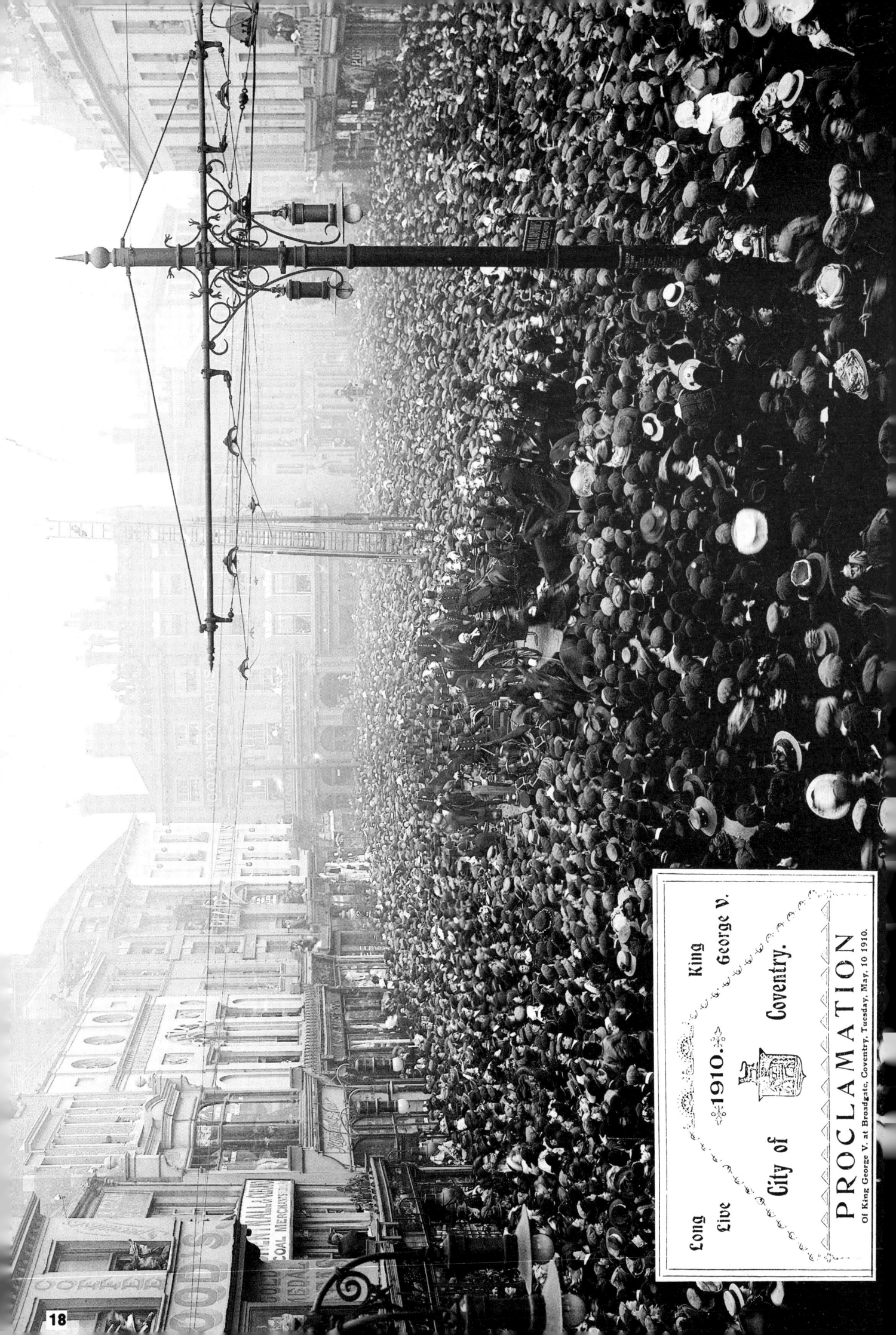

PROCLAMATION

Of King George V. at Broadgate, Coventry, Tuesday, May, 10 1910.

Long
Live
City of
Coventry.

King
George V.
1910.

Daimler staff, Coventry Drill Hall, c.1912

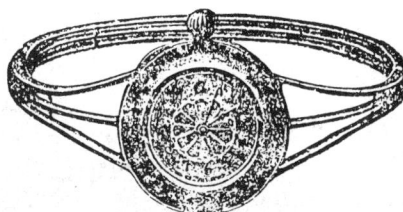

Members of the Coventry Police Force, the Watch Committee and officials, 1913. The famous Antarctic explorer, Edward Shackleton, sits with arms folded in the centre of the front row

Pool Meadow Fair, c.1913

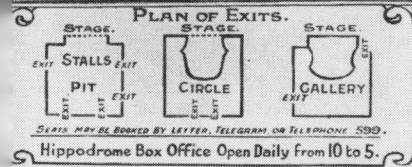

Maudslay bus, Walsgrave Road, 1914

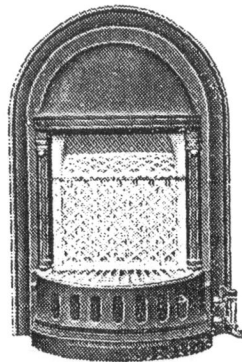

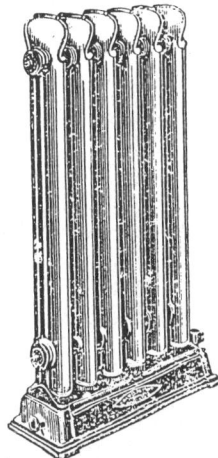

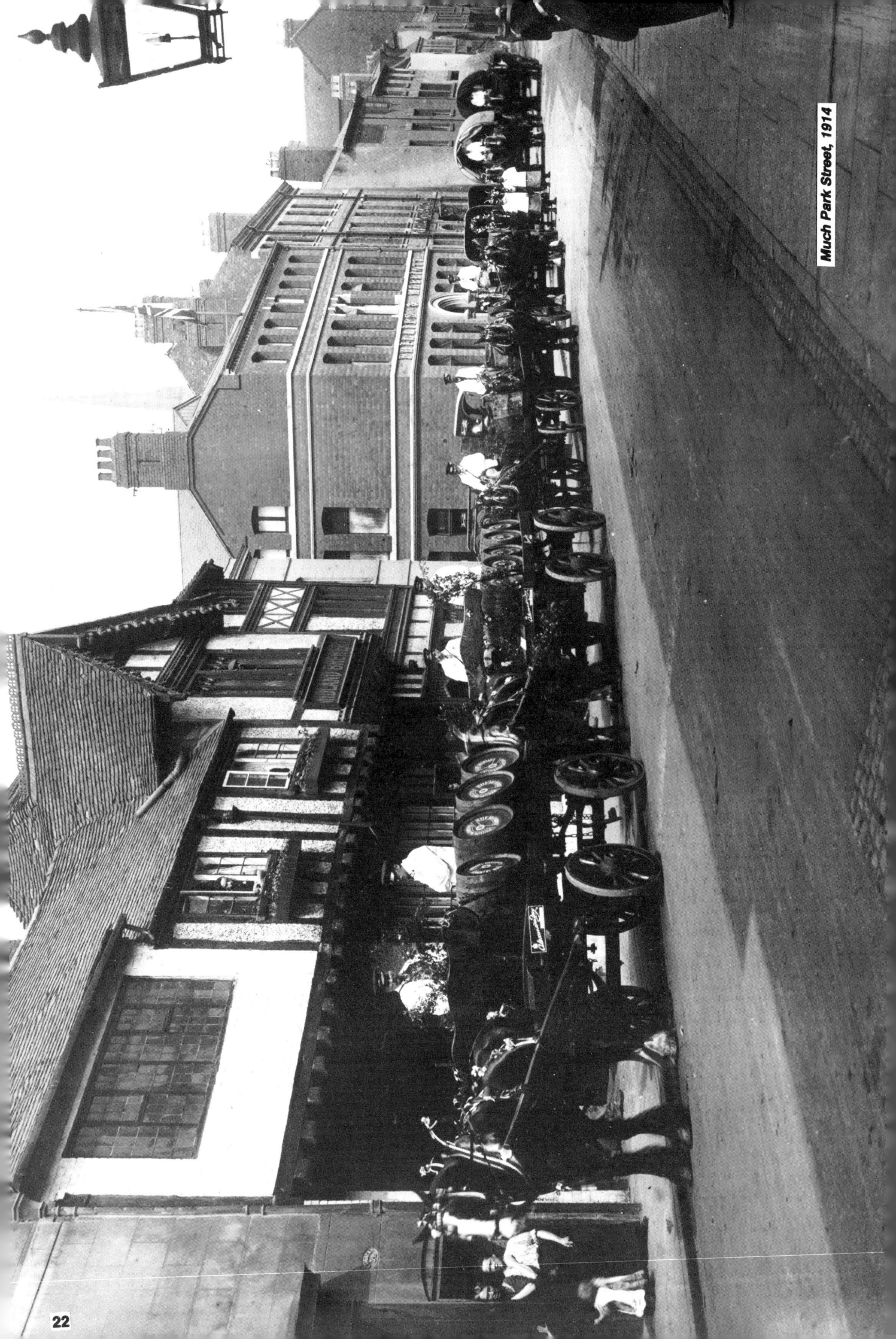

Much Park Street, 1914

The Churches. 1914

The scheme for the division of the diocese of Worcester by the separation of the county of Warwick, and the restoration and re-endowment of the old bishopric of Coventry, was practically accomplished in 1914, though a vigorous effort carried on in the early part of this year. A system of weekly collections was arranged; and at the end it was announced that about £40,000 had been collected. This with the sum already in hand, some outside benefactions, and interest, would be sufficient to meet expenses, and to provide the minimum of income for the bishop required by the law.

The movement for church extension in Coventry has made some progress during the year. The dedication of Earlsdon temporary church took place last December. The Rev. Louis Rogers, who has been Curate-in-charge of St. Margaret's parish since its formation, has been instituted its first vicar. The north aisle recently added to Radford Church was dedicated by the Archdeacon on Saturday, December 20th. The Parish Rooms and Sunday School, in connection with Christ Church were opened by Lord Cheylesmore on the 31st of January.

The assumption of pastorates in the city, during the year, of the Rev. Dr. Dakin and the Rev. F. M. Hirst has been an outstanding feature of Nonconformist life locally.

Tramcar with first woman conductor, 1915

TEA at 5 o'clock "Granville Arms."
GREENWICH TIME BALL.

Please adhere to the times of Programme.

DEPARTURE.

The Chara-a-bancs leave *The Autocar* Offices, Hertford St at 1.15 p.m. sharp.

Warwick 20 min. stay

RETURNING

At 8 p.m. prompt, *via* Warwick and Kenilworth, reach Coventry 10 p.m.

Kenilw'h 20 min. stay

ROUTE AND PLACES OF INTEREST.

Barford will be reached *via* Kenilworth Road, Green Lane, Finham Bridge, Ashow, Guy's Cliffe, Warwick (20 min. stay at "The Bowling Green"). The journey will be resumed over Warwick Castle Bridge (splendid view of Castle), along Banbury Road, New Waters to Barford. Here, Sherbourne Church, the River Avon, Barford Church and the picturesqueness of the village generally should find their share of admirers.

SWIMMING, CRICKET, QUOITS, SKITTLES. and other recreations may be indulged in.

GOD SAVE THE KING.

SMOKING CONCERT (Provisional).

CHAIRMAN	MR. H. ROLLINS.
PIANOFORTE SOLO	Fireman W. Swann.
SONG	Capt. G. H. Baker.
SONG	T. Rose.
SONG	Fireman W. Swann.
SONG	Fireman C. Yeoman.
TOAST THE FIRM	Capt. G. H. Baker. Respond Mr. H. Rollins.
SONG	R. Blay.
SONG	Fireman R. Perry.
SONG	Fireman W. Swann.
TOAST OUR VISITORS	Lieut. A. H. Howell. Respond Mr. R. Atkins.
SONG	T. Rose.
SONG	J. Salmon.
SONG	Fireman C. Yeoman.

6.6.14.

Munition workers pause from their job of filling shells, Ordnance Factory, Red Lane, 1914/18

Outing of wounded soldiers to Stoneleigh Deer Park, 1915

Staff of Coventry and Warwickshire Hospital with military patients, 1914/18

Soldiers mount guard outside the munitions factory of Hotchkiss & Co., Gosford Street, c.1916

Coventry Income Tax Office staff, c.1916

Queen Mary and the Princess Royal (in white) arrive at Coventry Station, September 18, 1917

Peace Celebrations, 1919
JULY 21, 1919.

PROVINCIAL towns and cities entered into the spirit of July 19, with great enthusiasm, and some wonderful pageants were witnessed.

Lady Godiva reappeared at Coventry— dressed; Banbury's Lady, with rings on her fingers and bells on her toes, rode to Banbury Cross on a white charger; Portsmouth and Plymouth saw portions of the Fleet gaily bedecked to celebrate the victory in which the Navy played such a great part.

WHEN THE NEWS IS RECEIVED IN COVENTRY

How City will Celebrate Conclusion of Armistice.

The following letter from the Mayor appeared in our columns on Saturday :—

Council House,
9th November, 1918.

Sir,—I shall be obliged if you will insert this letter in your issue to-night, so that the inhabitants may be acquainted with the arrangements which are being made officially for announcing to the public, when that news is received, that the armistice terms have been agreed to by Germany.

So soon as official notification has been received flags will be hoisted on St. Mary's Hall and the Council House, and the church bells will be rung. The Town Crier will also proclaim the news throughout the city.

If the news is received while the factories in the city are in work the syrens or hooters of the factories will be sounded at a given hour, and it is expected that for the remainder of that day and the day following a general holiday will be observed in all the industries of the city.

Arrangements will also be made for granting a holiday to all the school children.

I trust that this announcement will avoid any misunderstanding, and that the citizens will restrain themselves until the official notification is given.—Yours truly,

J. I. BATES, Mayor.

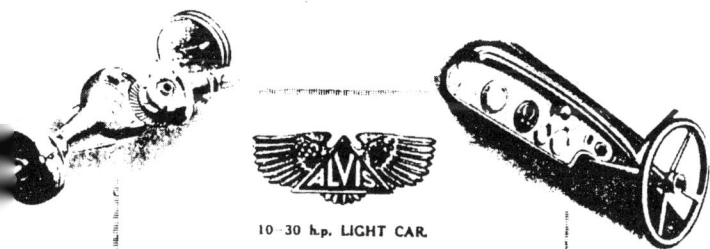

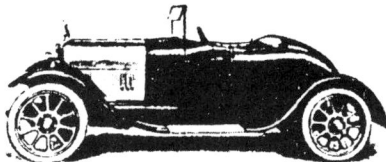

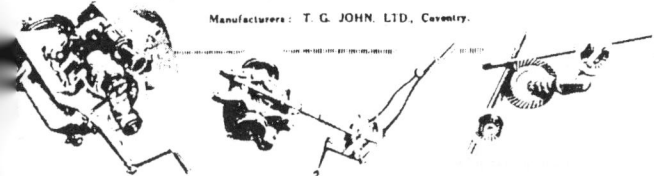

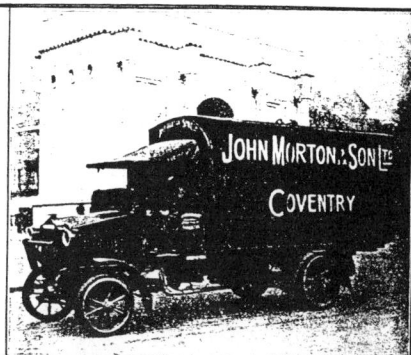

Souvenir
Programme

Official Opening & Dedication
of the War Memorial Park,
Saturday, July 9th, 1921.

By His Worship the Mayor (Councillor W. H. Grant),
and the Bishop of Coventry.

With the Compliments of the Baths and Parks Committee.

Daimler staff, 1922

Loading up the latest edition into Alvis vans, September 1924

Stoke Infants' School, 1925

Prototype Armstrong Whitworth Argosy, 1926

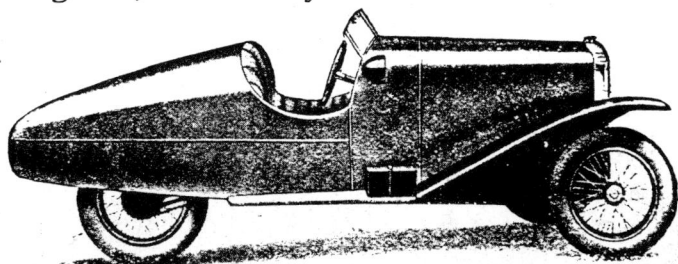

Chief Constable Imber and the Coventry Police, 1927

FIRST DAY OF GREAT STRIKE 5.5.26.

Not So Complete as Hoped by its Promoters

PREMIER'S AUDIENCE OF THE KING

Miners and the General Council Meet at House of Commons

Oliver Street, 1927. It was quite a common practice for a photographer to round up the local children, take a group picture and then visit their homes selling prints

CITY OF COVENTRY

ORDER OF CEREMONIAL
AT THE UNVEILING AND DEDICATION
OF THE
COVENTRY
WAR MEMORIAL
BY
FIELD-MARSHAL EARL HAIG
K.T., O.M., G.C.B., K.C.I.E., G.C.V.O.

ON

SATURDAY, 8th OCTOBER, 1927,
AT 3 P.M.

THIS MEMORIAL IS ERECTED BY THE CITIZENS
OF COVENTRY IN GRATEFUL REMEMBRANCE
OF THE 2,587 MEN OF COVENTRY WHO LAID
DOWN THEIR LIVES IN THE GREAT WAR.

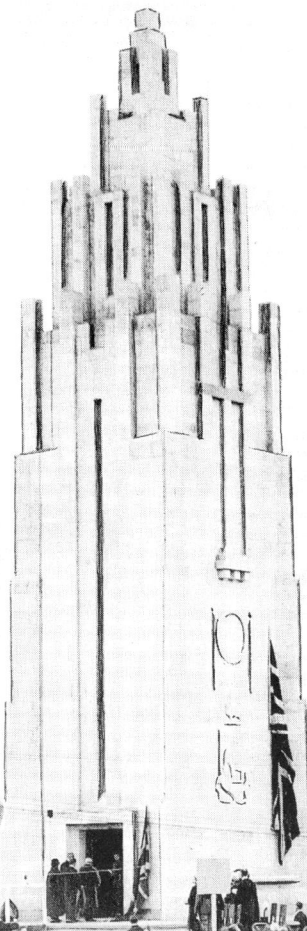

Armstrong Siddeley licence-built Pavesi (Italian) tractor for the War Office, Whitley Common, 1929

Priced from
£135

JUNIOR SALOON £160

The SINGER Junior
represents the most remarkable value in British light-car history

Each Model is a FULL SIZE light car with much more room and comfort than the usual "baby" car, and all Four-Seaters have FOUR WIDE DOORS, an important point to remember. There are six JUNIOR Models from which to choose, all fitted with four-wheel brakes, automatic screen wiper, speedometer, electric and bulb horns, and Newton hydro-pneumatic shock absorbers which make a wonderful difference to the riding comfort. Whichever Model suits your purpose best, you may be certain it is the biggest value you can buy. A personal examination and test will prove this to your satisfaction. SINGER & CO. Ltd., Coventry.

1929

Porlock Sports Model £140   Four-Seater Tourer £140

The Armstrong Siddeley 15 h.p. 6 cyl Fabric Saloon, price £360.

ARMSTRONG SIDDELEY
SIXES

THE NEW 15 H.P.   1929

THE ideal car for the Owner-Driver—especially the lady—the Armstrong Siddeley 15 h.p. Six is the best medium powered, full-sized family car on the road at a modest price.

Easy to drive, economical to run, simple to maintain. Handsome coachwork of first quality, fashioned on modern lines, attractive two-tone colour schemes.

Engine of Aircraft quality. Lively performance. Light steering. Perfect brakes.

You cannot buy better value. A trial run will convince you. Arrange one to-day. Cars on view at all our Agents.

Fabric Saloon, 6 lights   £360 complete
Coachbuilt Saloon, 6 lights   £395 complete

Write for Catalogue A54
ARMSTRONG SIDDELEY MOTORS LTD, COVENTRY
LONDON: 10 OLD BOND STREET, W.1
MANCHESTER: 35 KING STREET WEST
Agents in all principal towns

BUY BRITISH AND KEEP YOUR COUNTRYMEN EMPLOYED

Hertford Street, c.1929

THIS HOSPITAL WAS OPENED ON THE
28TH, JANUARY 1929,
BY THE
COUNTESS HAIG,
AS A BRANCH OF THE
COVENTRY & WARWICKSHIRE HOSPITAL
FOR THE TREATMENT OF CONVALESCENT PATIENTS

IT WAS DEDICATED BY THE
LORD BISHOP OF COVENTRY,
(THE RT. REV. LISLE CARR, D.D.)
AND NAMED
THE ALCOCK CONVALESCENT HOSPITAL.

IN MEMORY OF
JOHN ALCOCK
OF THE CITY OF COVENTRY
THROUGH WHOSE BENEFICENCE
THE HOSPITAL WAS OPENED.

CYRIL D. SIDDELEY, CHAIRMAN
WM. IVENS.   VICE-CHAIRMAN
(MISS) R. HOOPER.   SECRETARY.

Armstrong Siddeley Genet engines, c.1930

Croft Road, 1931

Cross Cheaping, c.1930

Burges, 1931

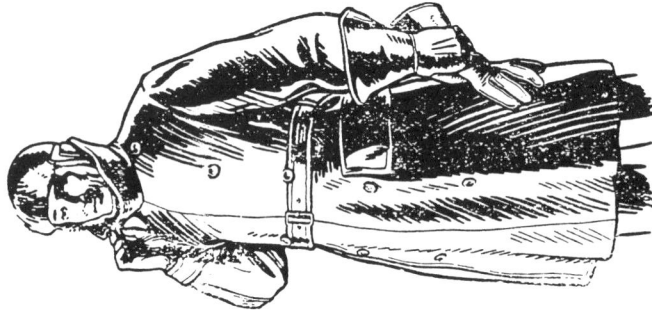

Greyfriars Green, August 27, 1933

Broadgate, August 27, 1933

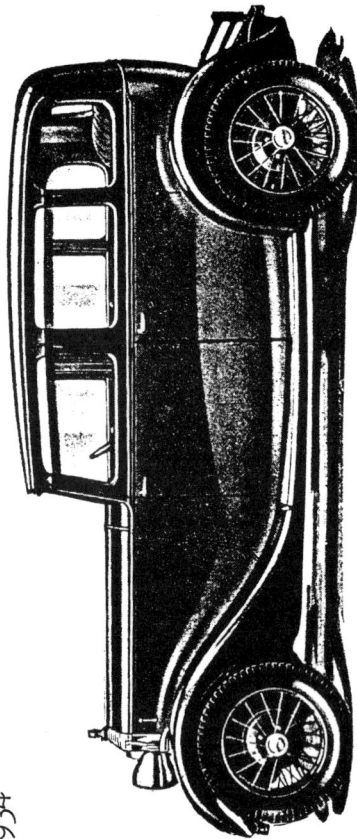

The CITY of COVENTRY

GENERAL INFORMATION 1934

Parliamentary Representation. Parliamentary Borough returns one Member, although, since the 1st April, 1928, parts then added still represented by members for three adjoining constituencies. Became a County Borough under Local Government Act in 1888.

Population. Population in 1901 was 69,978; in 1911, 106,349; in 1921, 128,157; 1931, 178,126 and 1933 (estimated) 182,000, having almost trebled itself in thirty-two years.

Railways. City has five stations, besides three for goods only. Frequent express trains to and from London by the L.M.S. Also good services to North and West. Branch lines to Kenilworth, Warwick and Leamington; and to Nuneaton, Leicester and Nottingham.

Road Distances from Coventry. To London, 90½ miles; Birmingham, 18; Nuneaton, 8½; Leicester, 24; Rugby, 12; Northampton, 28; Banbury, 27; Stratford-upon-Avon, 18; Kenilworth, 5¼; Warwick, 10¼.

Road Services. See page 18.

Parking Places. One central parking place at Pool Meadow in centre of city, within easy reach shopping centre and places of interest, capacity 500 cars; also Corporation Street; Priory Street (near the Cathedral); Spon End; Swanswell Place; Warwick Road (near Greyfriars Green).

Approaches. On the London Road by Dunchurch. Famous avenue, replanted as a War Memorial to the 29th Division. On the Kenilworth Road by another avenue of trees. From Nuneaton through North-east Warwickshire, and portion of George Eliot country.

Early Closing. Thursday. **Market Day.** Friday.

Hotels. King's Head (R.A.C., A.A.) and Queen's (R.A.C., listed A.A.), Hertford Street; London (non-licensed, R.A.C. appointed), see page 98; Warwick (non-licensed), Warwick Road; Rosslyn, Warwick Row; Fairhill, Warwick Road.

Banks. There are branches of Barclays, Lloyds, the Midland, National Provincial and Westminster Banks.

General Post Office. Latest times of posting for London at the Head Post Office: Monday to Friday, 11.30 p.m. Saturday, 9.30 p.m., Sunday, 11.0 p.m.

Rotary Club. Mondays, at Y.M.C.A., The Quadrant, at 1 p.m.

Cinemas, etc. *Alexandra Theatre*, Ford Street, continuous; *Broadway Cinema*, Albany Road, owned by F. & S. Cinemas Ltd. (see page 86), continuous; *Brookville*, Holbrook Lane, owned by Philpott Bros. & Orr (see facing page 84), matinée daily at 3 (Fridays excepted), continuous evenings from 6.30, Sundays at 8 p.m.; *Carlton Theatre*, Stoney Stanton Road, owned by Scala Entertainments Ltd. (see facing page 84), sound films (Western Electric), matinée daily at 3 (Fridays excepted), continuous evenings from 6.30, Sundays at 8 p.m., large free car park; *Crown Theatre*, Far Gosford Street, continuous, matinée daily; *Dovedale Cinema*, New Inn Bridge, Foleshill, continuous; *Empire Theatre*, Hertford Street, continuous; *Gaumont Palace*, continuous; *Globe Theatre*, Primrose Hill Street, continuous, matinée daily; *Grand Cinema* (see page 86), Foleshill Road, owned by F. & S. Cinemas Ltd., continuous; *Imperial*, continuous; *Lyric*, Holbrook Lane, matinée Mondays, Thursdays and Saturdays, evenings continuous; *Palladium*, *Picture House* (see facing page 84), matinée daily at 3, evenings and Saturdays continuous 6.30, Sundays at 8 p.m.; *Plaza Cinema* (see facing page 84), near L.M.S. station, matinées daily at 3, evenings and Saturdays continuous from 6.30, Sundays 8 p.m., best theatre for sound, comfort, etc., Nos. 8, 9, 10 and 11 buses pass the doors; *Prince of Wales Theatre*, Stoney Stanton Road, continuous; *Rialto* (see facing page 84), Radford's rendezvous, enjoys the proud reputation of always providing a good show at popular prices, large free car park; *La Scala* (see facing page 84), Far Gosford Street, continuous daily from 2.30, Sundays from 7.30 p.m. La Scala was opened in 1912 and although, therefore, one of the first to be opened in Coventry, it has always progressed with the times and possesses the finest Western Electric sound equipment and lighting effects machine. Magnascopic screen, atmosphere purifying apparatus and large car park, have been added to make a visit to La Scala thoroughly enjoyable.

Newspapers and Periodicals. *Coventrian*, three times a year, 1/-, King Henry VIII School, Coventry; *Coventry ABC Railway Rates Book*, quadrennially, £4 3s., Railway & Shipping Publishing Co. Ltd., 12 Cherry Street, Birmingham 1/-; *Coventry Chronicle, Bedworth & Foleshill News*, Saturday, 2d.; *Coventry Engineering Society Journal*, monthly on 15th, 1/-; *Coventry Herald*, Friday and Saturday, 2d.; *Coventry Standard*, Friday and Saturday, 2d.; *Midland Daily Telegraph*, 1d.; *Coventry Stock & Share List*, monthly on 1st, gratis, T. M. Daffern, 19 and 20 High Street, Coventry.

Butcher Row, just prior to demolition for the creation of Trinity Street, 1935

Freedom of City For Lord Nuffield and Mr. H. R. Farren

1936

First Dual Election To Coveted Roll

COVENTRY City Council, meeting to-day in special session within the ancient Guildhall of St. Mary's, conferred the highest honour in their power upon Lord Nuffield and Mr. Hugh R. Farren, when, for the first time, two enrolments were made upon the same day in the very exclusive Roll of Honorary Freemen.

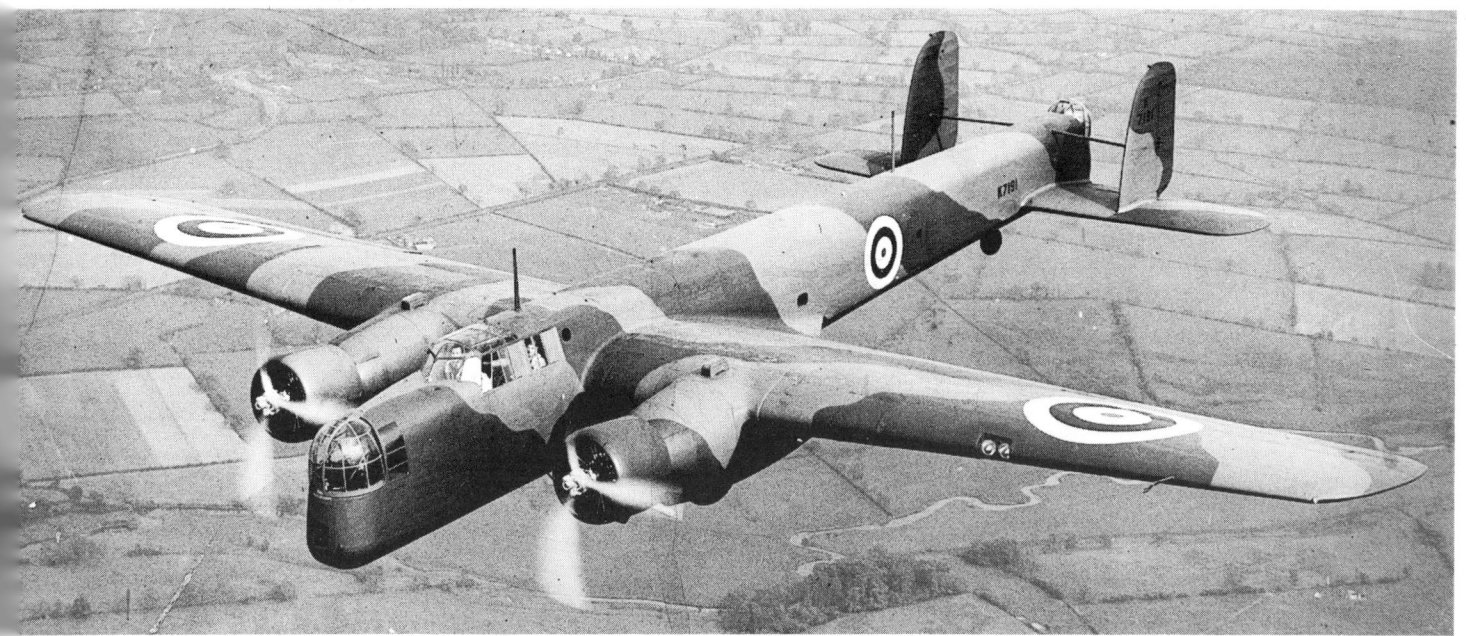

Armstrong Whitworth, "Whitley Mk I" c.1935

41

Modern Machine Tools Ltd
Harmonica Band, c.1936

Modern Machine Tools Ltd
FC, c.1936

Modern Machine Tools Ltd
Carnival entry, c.1935. M.D.
Harry Weston (who later
became a Mayor of
Coventry) can be seen,
wearing a bow-tie, in the
background

Frances Burchell, in the guise of Lady Godiva, Stoney Stanton Road, 1936

Folly Lane Junior School, 1936

KING EDWARD HAS MADE HIS DECISION. HE
IS TO GIVE UP THE THRONE.

10.12.36.

MR. BALDWIN ANNOUNCED THIS DECISION TO A
CROWDED HOUSE OF COMMONS THIS AFTERNOON

Armstrong Siddeley pneumatic-tyred railcar, 1936

The new Hippodrome, 1937. The old Hippodrome is on the right

Warwick Lane, 1937

Broadgate, 1937

The Midland Daily Telegraph

Coronation Supplement

WEDNESDAY, MAY 12, 1937

OUR KING & QUEEN: LONG MAY THEY REIGN

CORONATIONS OF OLD

Some Splendid Pageantry

THE ANCIENT RITUAL

(BY BERNARD DAWKINS)

THE CORONATION is the formal public ratification of accession, which dates from the death of the previous monarch. This does not mean that a Sovereign is not properly King until the date of his Coronation. His succession is immediate upon the death of his predecessor—"Le Roi est mort, vive le Roi."

In earlier times, when conditions in the country were less stable, the new King often felt he was not secure until he was crowned. So the interval between accession and crowning was shorter than now. It was actually the case during the reign of Henry II that the heir-apparent was crowned during his father's lifetime in order to prevent any possible squabble as to the accession.

FEAR OF NEW CLAIMANT

To-day the interval between accession and crowning is over a year. It was far shorter with the earlier Georges, as there was always a fear that a Stuart might appear as a claimant. George I was crowned only eleven weeks after his accession. George II after four months. King Edward VII was crowned nineteen months after the death of his predecessor, but the ceremony had [...]

MONARCH & PEOPLE

Safeguard of Liberty: Link of Empire

THRONE THAT DESCENDS FROM LEGENDARY DAYS

(BY LORD DUNSANY)

THE Crown is so much a part of the story of the British Isles that any attempt to write upon kingship in this country is to intrude upon nothing less than English history.

From the romantic edges of legend the Crown has been borne to our day; and the deep grief that has been felt at the loss of King Edward, the shadow that seemed to be hanging over the land while the issue was yet unknown, are indications that show clearly enough how interwoven are the roots of the monarchy among the heart-strings of the British race. Above that shadow [...]

the ruins. What would have happened to our credit, and, indeed, our solvency, but for that, I cannot say, but there remains widespread through the Empire a dim feeling of gratitude to King George V for some great peril averted on that occasion. It is not the only occasion for which his people felt grateful, when their sentiments welled up into one loyal feeling that was manifest on the day of the Silver Jubilee.

Loyalty to the King is an emotion, and cannot, therefore, be easily explained nor need be defended; while to specify the advantages that we loyal subjects derive from it seems almost sacrilegious. And yet it is upon loyalty, I feel convinced, that depend such things as the price of bread remaining near its present figure, and not going to a pound a loaf or even twenty pounds. Such fantastic figures, and even wilder, madder ones than that, have been found in other lands when change came suddenly, and the rocking of troubled thrones have before now put the price of bread beyond the scope of ordinary men, and these ordinary men have starved in millions, before now, in other lands.

TO THE ENDS OF THE EARTH

An honoured reigning family stands between us and many a misery of which we have never thought, and need not think. It does not prevent change where change is beneficent, and indeed the King's signature is the instrument [...]

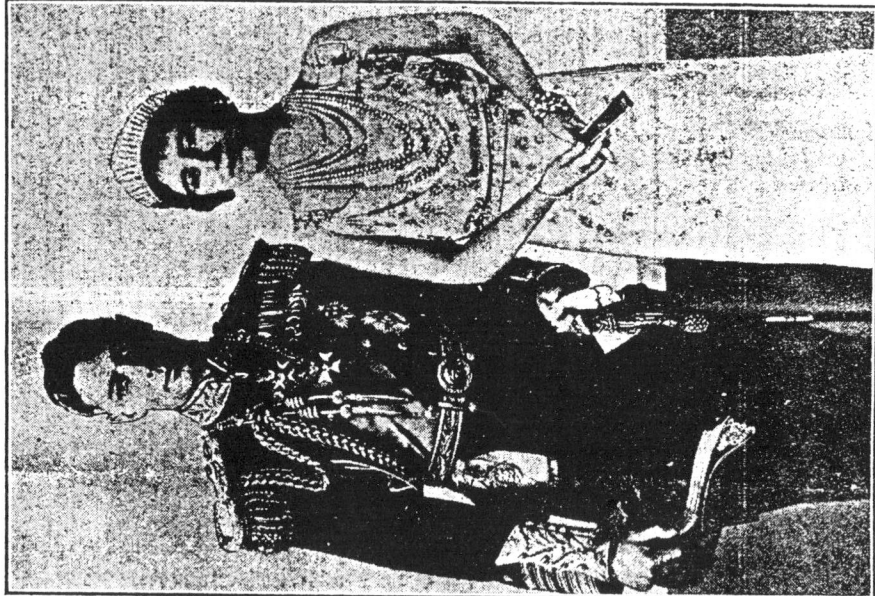

WHERE KINGS ARE CROWNED

Abbey's History of 1,000 Years

FROM SEBERT THE SAXON TO GEORGE VI

(BY J. W. HOPPEN, F.S.A.)

WESTMINSTER ABBEY has been the recognised scene of our Coronation ceremonies at least from the time of William the Conqueror, and from his day all England's rulers, except two, have been crowned within the Abbey Church. The exceptions are Edward V and Edward VIII, neither of whom was ever crowned. The former was one of the unfortunate little princes who were murdered in the Tower.

Westminster's rise to fame was as remarkable as it was rapid.

When Edward the Confessor came to the throne in 1042, the Abbey was dilapidated and poor, with but a small number of monks. But east of it, between the precincts and the river, stood a new palace, the building of which had probably been begun about 40 years earlier. This became the Confessor's favourite residence.

Throughout the reign of Canute an exile in Normandy, and during that period had vowed that should he ever attain to the throne of his ancestors he would make a pilgrimage of thanksgiving to the tomb of St. Peter at Rome.

held, was simply doing a wise thing in arranging for his crowning in the new church which the pious King had built. For he claimed that Edward had named him as his rightful successor. On the other side it may be said that, if the Conqueror had heard of the Confessor's alleged wish that Westminster should be the scene of future coronations there was still stronger reason for his choice of it.

However the tradition arose it has certainly existed from a very early date, and been strictly adhered to throughout our history.

We may turn now to the Palace, which was also growing in importance. During the last few years of the Confessor, William the Conqueror built the Great Hall which still remains, it was not, perhaps, a very [...]

CORONATION FASHIONS

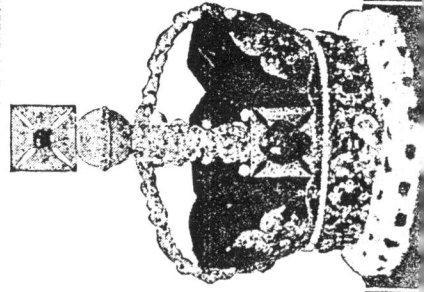

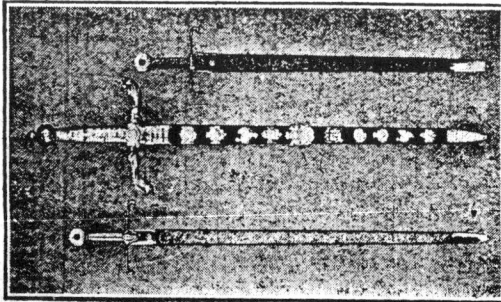

AIMS OF £1,570,000 FIVE-YEAR PROGRAMME

3 JAN 1939

"We have the opportunity to-day to lay the foundations of a new Coventry," was the description of one speaker at Coventry City Council to-day, regarding the programme of proposed capital expenditure for the next five years which the Policy Advisory Committee sponsored.

Alderman W. E. Halliwell was the mover of the recommendation which included projects totalling £1,570,000 in cost for the five years, and also a proposal that the general rate for the city for 1939-40 should include a sum equivalent to the proceeds of a 6d. rate to be applied in meeting the annual debt charges in respect of the capital programme.

Alderman O. M. Flint moved the reference back, stating that the carrying out of the programme would mean, not a sixpenny increase in the rates, but one of 2s., because it would be an increase of 6d. a year for four years.

Alderman Fred Lee said he thought more time should be given for members to consider the programme in detail, and other speakers supported this view, but the amendment was lost by 24 votes to 30. The recommendation was carried by 29 votes to 25.

Alderman T. J. Harris then moved that the rate for the coming year be increased from 13s. to 13s. 6d., and remarked that the amount needed to be raised was £1,137,131. Mr. Lee Gordan seconded.

An amendment that the rate should be maintained at 13s. was defeated, and the recommendation carried.

A COVENTRY CHRISTMAS TREE

A thirty-feet high Christmas tree was set up in Broadgate, Coventry, yesterday by the Corporation. The tree, an evergreen from a Corporation plantation, will be illuminated by the Corporation Electricity Department. It was set up following a suggestion made by Alderman O. M. Flinn.

24.12.37.

STILL CAPABLE OF BEING DRIVEN.

16 MAR 1938

PLANS FOR REMOVAL.

Nineteen years after Coventry's war-time tank was driven on to its concrete base at Grey Friars Green, where it has remained ever since, Mr. L. D. Edwards, of the Daimler Motor Co., yesterday unlocked the padlocked door and inside found the 125-h.p. engine in perfect condition.

After an inspection, lasting only a minute or so, he was able to assure himself that the moving of the tank—a proposal recently put forward—could be effected under its own power.

A month or so ago the Coventry Baths and Parks Committee suggested that the tank should be sold for scrap. This led to an outcry by

WEDNESDAY, SEPTEMBER 8, 1937.

EMPLOYMENT EXTRAORDINARY

During the week ending August 23, in the midst of what was formerly regarded as one of Coventry's "slack periods," there were only 2,510 totally unemployed persons on the books of the city's Employment Exchange. There were a further 1,208 men and women temporarily suspended, but these people cannot be described as "unemployed," in the normally-accepted sense of the word. There are something like 110,000 insured workers in the Coventry area, so that the ratio of real unemployment works out at approximately 2¼ per cent. This is one of the most remarkable returns ever recorded, for those 2¼ per cent. of unemployed people include all those who are physically handicapped, the elderly, and the "square pegs in round holes," comprising a class of society that presents a permanent problem under any system of commercial organisation, and one that is common to every nation.

Broadgate, c.1938

49

No. 3 vehicle, Coventry & Warwickshire Hospital Saturday Fund ambulance, 1939

"The complement of H.M.S. Coventry expresses sympathy with the citizens in their adversity, and assures them that the ship will endeavour to repay" her Commander wired. In reply, the Mayor has said: "The city is deeply grateful for your telegram, and we know H.M.S. Coventry will carry out its word."

Women's Institute, Keresley & Coundon Produce Show, 1938

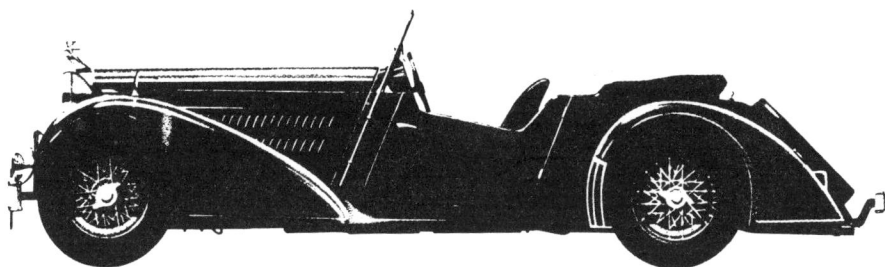

1939 ALVIS 4·3-LITRE TOURER by Vanden Plas. Owner: R. A. Parker, Esquire. Road tested by *The Autocar*, this car gave a mean average maximum speed of 100·84 m.p.h.

KPC 362

ALVIS

KPC 362

51

WARWICKSHIRE MAN'S DIARY

19.2.40

18, Hertford Street,
Coventry.
Tuesday morning.

SALUTATIONS to Coventry's business people.

With half a chance they would have made yesterday quite an ordinary working day. Many, of course, managed it, but I am thinking particularly of those whose ordinary every day tasks are located in the central business area.

It did my heart good to see how they arrived to carry on among the ruins of so much that they had loved. How disappointed they were when they had to be prevented from entering areas in which there were unsafe buildings.

"But I work up there," was a complaint one heard even from the lips of mild city typists when officialdom stepped in to thwart them. They all wanted to be back on the job.

It is in moments like these that that certain traditional something in the British spirit comes to the fore. Hitler hasn't even started to realise what he is up against.

Sorting out the devastation in pawnbroker's shop, October 21, 1940

Broadgate/High Street looking towards Trinity Street, November 15, 1940

Coventry Blitz

1940, November 16: Thursday night's attack on Coventry was characterised by the fiercest example of ruthless and indiscriminate destruction the Nazi bombers have given outside London. Five hundred enemy planes made the series of attacks. Casualties totalled 1,000 and hundreds lost their homes Of the Cathedral, walls and spire only were left standing The main body of the 14th-century perpendicular architecture was reduced to ruins Two other churches and a number of public buildings, business and residential premises—the larger part of the heart of the city—were damaged or swept away. Coventry people bore the ordeal with great courage. [Two days after the raid the King toured the ruined city]

COVENTRY BOMB SEARCH GOES ON

BOMB disposal investigation in Coventry has resulted in two reports being discredited recently, and a third shaft is now in its final stages without any trace of a bomb yet.

German prisoners-of-war who are pursuing this work under the supervision of British N.C.O.s, found bomb fins in a shaft they had made in the garden of 27, Gun Lane, Stoke. At a depth of 13 feet they traced a tunnel, but this petered out, and it was concluded that the bomb must have exploded underground.

STOKE EXCAVATION

The investigations at a site in London Road cemetery were begun after workmen who were clearing ivy from the gardens found a clear hole beneath. This report has been discredited after a thorough search.

The only site now being excavated is in a garden at Shakespeare Street, Stoke. A shaft has been made, without any sign of a bomb, however.

The squad have one new report to examine in Coventry —in a garden at Allesley Old Road.

GEC Salvage Squad at the ready, 1942

THE SCORCHED EARTH POLICY, FOR WORKERS

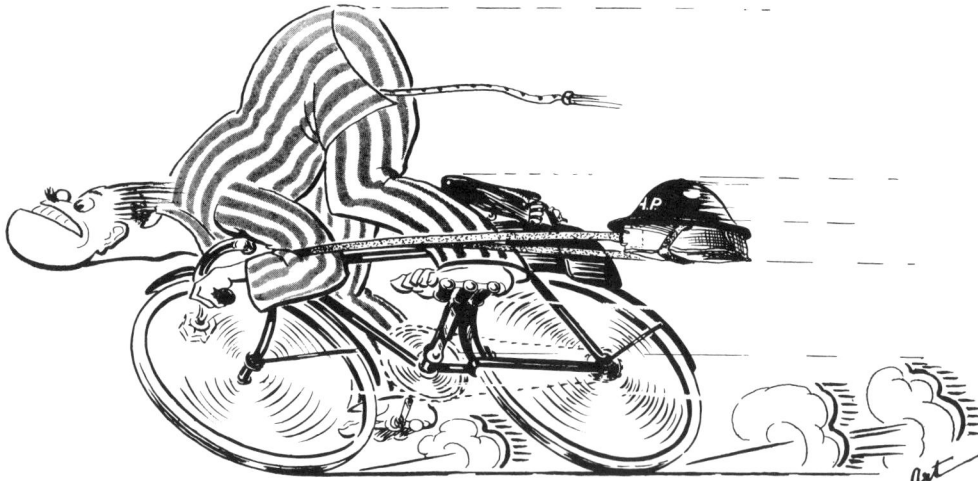

GET THERE ON TIME !

THE HOME GUARD.

This group consists of about half of a Company of a Warwickshire Battalion of the Home Guard, made up of the personnel of one of The British Thomson-Houston Company's factories.

A number of members could not be present when the photograph was taken.

This Company has done very well in training, and has recently been awarded the Battalion Proficiency Cup.

The officers seen in the group are Major R. Poole, commanding the Company (*sitting, front centre*); on his right Lieuts. Pallett and Thorneycroft, and on his left Lieut. Parrott and 2nd Lieut. Crouch.

1942

"OUR TASK WILL NOT BE EASY .."

YOU'RE TELLING ME !

ANY BRISTLES ?

The Ministry of Supply is taking a census of stocks of bristles in the United Kingdom at the close of business to-day. Any person or firm who has in his possession or custody any bristles, and who has not received a form should write to the Ministry of Supply, R.M.2C., Warwick.

The Coventry Evening Telegraph

Proprietors: Midland Daily Telegraph Ltd
Hertford Street. Telephone 5011.
No. 16,527 (54th Year).   TUESDAY, JUNE 6, 1944.   THREE HALFPENCE

OVER THERE! DAWN LANDINGS IN NORTHERN FRANCE

Paratroops in Action After Great Sea & Air Bombardment

"COMMUNIQUE NUMBER ONE" SET THE WORLD AGOG TO-DAY. IT WAS ISSUED FROM SUPREME HEADQUARTERS ALLIED EXPEDITIONARY FORCE (SHAEF FOR SHORT) AT 9.33 A.M. AND SAID:

"UNDER THE COMMAND OF GENERAL EISENHOWER ALLIED NAVAL FORCES SUPPORTED BY STRONG AIR FORCES BEGAN LANDING ALLIED ARMIES THIS MORNING ON THE NORTHERN COAST OF FRANCE."

THE LANDINGS, IT IS UNDERSTOOD, WERE MADE IN NORMANDY BETWEEN 6 A.M. and 8.15 A.M.

The Allies have established beachheads in Northern France and are slashing inland, according to photo reconnaissance pilots back from the landings, says a Reuter message to-day from the Eighth U.S.A.A.F. photo reconnaissance base.

A confident Mr. Churchill, in the House of Commons to-day, underlined the confident comments of the Allied Generals in his necessarily brief review of the landings. "There are already hopes that actual tactical surprise has been attained and we hope to furnish the enemy with a succession of surprises during the course of the fighting," he said. Mr. Churchill's statement appears on page 8.

A military observer who landed with the first assault troops has described how wave upon wave of infantrymen surged up the beaches, overcoming any opposition in their way and surging on.

General Dwight D. Eisenhower, "Ike" to Mr. Churchill and the American Army, Supreme Allied Commander, is 53. Responsible for training of U.S. forces in Britain since January, 1942.

General Sir Bernard Montgomery, C.-in-C. British group of Armies. "Monty" to Army, and "Calculating Machine" to Germans

Air Chief Marshal Sir Arthur Tedder, Deputy Supreme Allied Commander, first airman to be No. 2 in command of combined naval, Army and air forces, is a Scot, aged 53.

Admiral Sir Bruce Fraser, commanding Home Fleet, was in flagship Duke of York at sinking of the Scharnhorst. Has been described as Navy's greatest gunner. Aged 55.

BERLIN SAYS ALLIES IN JERSEY AND GUERNSEY

BEHIND the bald announcement is the story of eventful hours crammed with radio flashes, the roar of countless bombers streaming towards the Continent, jubilation and speculation in the cities and villages.

W. E. West, Press Association correspondent at S.H.A.E.F., says that General Montgomery is in charge of the Army group carrying out the assault with British, Canadian and U.S. forces under his command.

Allied bombers roaring over at dawn gave British people the first hint that big events were under way. Almost simultaneously the B.B.C.'s French transmissions began to warn French people to get away from coastal areas, to avoid roads, railways and bridges. "Do not gather in large groups," added the message.

Latest German claims are that British and American prisoners have been taken, that at least four Anglo-American parachute and airborne divisions are engaged, and that a "big Allied warship" has been set on fire.

The landings were made on the Normandy coast and airborn troops took part in the operation. The Germans had earlier reported on their radio that airborne troops had been landed at the mouth of the Seine.

Germans Kept Guessing for Months

The place of the attack had kept the Germans guessing for months, but their heaviest defences had been prepared at the point of the shortest Channel crossings

Before our troops could land at various times between 6 and 8.15 this morning our minesweepers had to sweep the waters off the coast, other craft had to deal with underwater obstacles, and bombarding ships had to get into position to engage the coast defence guns.

It is hoped that the resistance groups in France will give the Germans an uncomfortable time with communications.

The bombing of railways and bridges will make it difficult for the Germans to move reserves. He will have to move the bulk of his troops by road, where the R.A.F. will probably be able to take a heavy toll.

The weather was not very kind on the continent and there may have been some sea sickness.

Over 640 Naval Guns Bombed Beaches

Supreme Headquarters, Allied Expeditionary Force, states that over 640 naval guns, from 16in. to 4in. are bombarding the beaches and enemy strong points in support of the armies.

Experience has shown that the destructive effect of naval bombardment, combined with extreme accuracy when effectively directed, has a great effect on enemy morale as well as heartening our troops.

Larger warships are mainly used for indirect fire and destroyers for engaging selected targets such as tanks, pillboxes, and machine-gun nests.

As the assault troops go ashore, forward observation posts are established by the Royal Regiment of Artillery. Indirect fire from the ships is directed by the observation officers at selected enemy strong-points, while visible targets ahead of our troops are engaged directly. Enemy batteries are engaged by indirect fire from the heavier warships controlled either by air observation or the "forward observers'" bombardment, who can direct the fire of individual bombarding ships and also call for additional fire power from

the naval commander as necessary.

Fighter-Bombers are Hitting Hard

Since the invasion began Allied fighter-bombers have been dive-bombing, glide-bombing and strafing German defences and communications. They are hitting any target that has a bearing on the strength of the German armies at the front. They fly literally into the mouths of guns and dive within feet of the spans which hold bridges together.

Situation Seems to be Going Well

Gault McGowan, representing the combined British Press, reporting from an English airfield after watching the invasion start from the air, said to-day:

The situation seems to be going well. The Luftwaffe has not yet put in an appearance in strength and the masses of manœuvre on both sides are moving into position.

Before returning I flew for miles inland, but saw no German armoured divisions on the move.

The air umbrella exceeded Dieppe. No outfit seemed without its cover. There was so many of us in the air that we had to get up there by coming (Continued on Back Page)

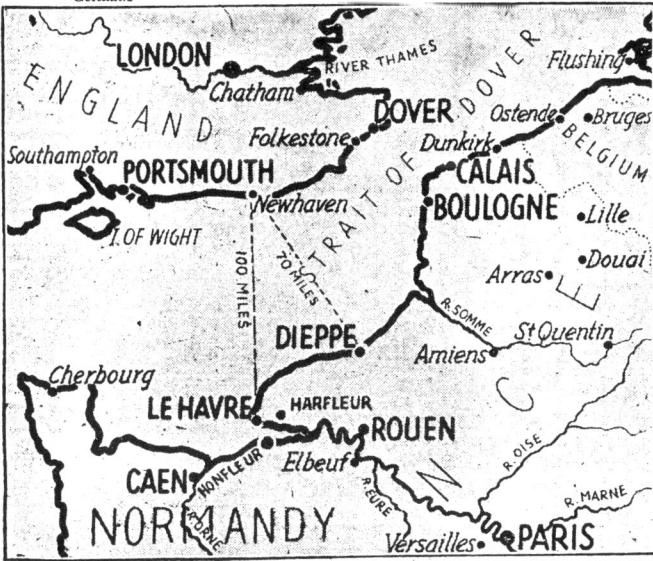

(Continued on Back Page)

Airborne Landings in Normandy in Great Depth —Berlin

ANGLO-AMERICAN airborne landings in Normandy have been made in great depth, says the German News Agency, which adds that fierce fighting is taking place at Caen.

Reuter's military correspondent learns that Hitler is taking personal command of all antiinvasion operations. He is surrounded by a staff, including four Marshals, and is believed to have moved his headquarters to a place somewhere in Northern France.

HITLER'S VERSION
A special announcement issued by official quarters in Berlin to-day said:—

"The long-expected attack by the British and Americans on the coast of Northern France began last night.

"A few minutes after midnight the enemy landed airborne formations in the area of the Seine Bay, simultaneously making heavy bombing attacks.

"Shortly afterwards numerous enemy landing boats protected by heavy Allied naval units approached the coast on other sectors.

"The German defenders were nowhere taken by surprise; they immediately took up the fight with the greatest energy.

"The parachute troops were partly engaged as they came down and the enemy ships were taken under effective fire whilst still on the high seas.

"Many parachute units were wiped out or taken prisoner; others were torn to pieces by exploding mines.

"In spite of constant violent air battles and heavy bombardment from the enemy ships the guns of the Atlantic Wall immediately intervened in the fighting. They scored hits on battleships and on landing craft, screened from view by smoke.

(Continued on Back Page)

(Continued on Back Page)

LATE NEWS

BERLIN EXPECTS NEW LANDINGS
The Berlin military spokesman said: "It is quite possible that within the next hours or days the focal point of the battle will shift to another sector of the French

THE AIRBORNE TROOPS
It is learned at Supreme H.Q. A.E.F. that the aircraft conveying the airborne troops did then job and got back without very heavy casualties.

Dutch children arrive in the city, from Eindhoven, for a "rehabilitation holiday", February 12 1945

VE-Day celebrations, Glencoe Road, 1945

The Red Cross and St. John

From Lord Iliffe.

13.5.45.

Sir,—In view of the large number of enquiries I am receiving as to whether further contributions are necessary now the need to provide food parcels for our prisoners of war in Europe no longer exists, I shall be glad if you will allow me to explain the position.

It is essential that the organisation must continue its beneficent work until the war in the Far East comes to an end and until its post-war responsibilities—which are considerable—have been taken care of.

The service to prisoners of war is only a section of the work, though a most important one. If sufficient funds are collected it is possible for the appeal to be discontinued although the War Organisation itself continues to function, and this will, in fact, take place when it is clear beyond all reasonable doubt that there is enough money in hand to meet the cost of the continued activities of the Organisation and its post-war responsibilities.

Until then I am asking that there shall be no falling off in the support we are receiving.

ILIFFE,
Chairman, Duke of Gloucester's Red Cross and St. John Fund.
St. James's Palace, S.W.1.

The Prime Minister, the Rt Hon Winston Churchill, acknowledges the crowd's greetings in Trinity Street, June 25, 1945

A service in the ruined nave of the Cathedral, c.1945

The first post-war Jaguar comes off the finishing line, September 1945

Argentinians inspect the first post-war Humber Snipe at the Coventry factory, September 24, 1945

The car, made in Coventry by the Humber Hillman Co., that took Field Marshal Montgomery on his triumphant journey from El Alamein across the desert and right up into Italy, is returned to the city by the War Office. Some of the original workers inspect it again, December 14, 1945

The Council of the Freemen's Guild, December 1946

Hillman line, Ryton-on-Dunsmore, 1946

The March Past of the Royal Warwickshire Regt. at the Council House, May 31, 1947. The Freedom of the City had earlier been conferred upon the regiment in the Memorial Park, when the Mayor, Ald. G. Briggs, presented the Deed of Privilege to their Colonel-in-Chief, Field Marshal Viscount Montgomery

ONE-WAY TRAFFIC SYSTEM PROPOSED

27 NOV 1947

CONFIRMATION SOUGHT FOR COVENTRY ORDER

GYRATORY SYSTEM TO REMOVE CONGESTION

An order to introduce a one-way traffic system in the centre of Coventry is about to be made by the Corporation and submitted to the Ministry of Transport for confirmation.

This sytem is bound up with the provision of the big traffic island which has been under construction in Broadgate since the spring.

It cannot be completed until the shops in certain badly bomb damaged buildings and in temporary premises in Smithford Street, have been transferred to new temporary premises in Broadgate, now nearing completion.

VISIT OF

HER ROYAL HIGHNESS
THE PRINCESS ELIZABETH

SATURDAY
22ND MAY, 1948

Coventry Old Contemptibles, Gosford Green, July, 1948

22.10.49.

Mrs. Douglas Unveils Lady Godiva Statue

As the bells of Coventry Cathedral boomed the hour of noon to-day, Mrs. Lewis W. Douglas, wife of the American Ambassador to Britain, unveiled, in the centre of Coventry's garden-island in Broadgate, the city's first adequate memorial — a 19ft. high bronze equestrian statue—to its benefactress, Lady Godiva.

This £20,000 gift by Mr. W. H. Bassett-Green, an 80-year-old native of the city now living at Winchcombe, near Cheltenham, linked the old Coventry with the new, said Mrs. Douglas, speaking to a crowded Broadgate. Its unveiling was a happy omen for the continuing reconstruction of Coventry.

The cue for the timing of the actual unveiling was provided by Tennyson in his poem, "Godiva." Her eleventh-century ride, naked, through Coventry's streets to remove from a burdened people a tax imposed by her husband, Earl Leofric, ended, Tennyson wrote, as:—

"With twelve great shocks of sound, the shameless noon

Was clash'd and hammer'd from a hundred towers, One after one . . . . "

Station Welcome

Mrs. Douglas was welcomed at Coventry railway station by the Mayoress (Mrs. V. A. Hammond), Mrs. J. Howat (wife of the Deputy Mayor) and Mr. H. A. Went (stationmaster), and received a bouquet from five-year-old Vicki Hammond, eldest of the Mayor's grandchildren.

On arrival at the Council House she was welcomed by the Mayor (Alderman V. A. Hammond) and introduced to Mr. Bassett-Green, Sir William Reid Dick (sculptor of the statue) and Lady Reid Dick, Dr. H. C. Schoch (First Secretary to the Netherlands Embassy in London) and Mrs. Schoch.

Cheylesmore Secondary Modern Boys' School F.C., 1950

Fancy dress at the Gaumont Cinema Saturday Morning Junior Club, c.1951

Smithford Street, January 25, 1950

63

WOMEN AND THE HOME

The cry for more and more is persistent

It is not just tea which is strictly rationed and price controlled, there is a world shortage of nearly everything people want for their health and comfort.

Our women folk are hard put to making things spin out—one of the most patriotic things they can do these days.

They have done it before and know what it means, bless 'em.

What to do to Acquire the Paris 1951 Look

[By a Special Correspondent]

PARIS.

THE French fashion shows are now in full swing, and as usual buyers from all over the world have rushed to the capital for news of what the masters of the French couture have created.

Shall we have long skirts, short skirts, fullness or austerity? Shall we, as a few years ago, have to discard all our previous dresses or frantically lengthen their skirts?

Here is the answer: "Bring out your old new-look dresses, shorten their skirts to mid-calf, add a fresh lawn or piqué collar, and you will have the 1951 Paris Look."

But a word of warning: Do not be tempted to overload your dresses with bows, ruffles, and petticoats. The new line will swing as you walk, but its swing will depend on beautiful cut, which will not rely on pads, frills, and furbelows.

Gilbert Orcel's honey-coloured straw embroidered in gold thread.

Maud et Nano make the youthful white boater, trimmed with a black rose and fine veiling, shown in the top picture. A black leghorn with ribbon streamers, also by Gilbert Orcel, is shown below.

No Restraint

Summer dresses will appeal to the young who like to be able to swing gracefully into the room and do not appear at their best when they are forced to trip with tiny steps restrained by hobble skirts.

Cristal or sun-ray pleating is used in profusion, in delightful spotted silks, thin shantungs, chiffons or organzas; this pleating is very fine and swings out gaily between flared panels, or bursts out at the back from an apron front. It has to be used generously and is often held slightly out by a moderately full taffeta petticoat. Jean Desses showed this apron effect in nearly all of his dresses.

Spring suits are usually beautifully and simply tailored, with straight skirts 14 inches from the ground and slightly squared shoulders. Jackets often button at the waist, which is still tightly nipped in: Pockets draw attention to the hips and help to accentuate the smallness of the waist.

British Material

It is encouraging to see many British materials used in the collections. Jacques Fath and Desses have a lovely shantung which is actually made of half pure silk and half nylon yarn, which gives it the shimmering effect so popular for afternoon dresses.

Beige, grey, cinnamon, cream merging to yellow, and, of course, black and navy with white are the main colours on the couturiers' palettes.

I was amused to hear the remark of my next-door neighbour: "Take some milk chocolate, throw in lots of whipped cream, add cellophane." and you have the new smart colour for this summer."

Hats Make News

As detailed drawings of dress collections are not allowed till the general public is admitted to view the new fashions on March 1, hats are the centre of interest.

The Frenchwoman has always been more hat-conscious than we are, but the new Paris hats are quite lovely and should encourage us to discard our wartime legacy of head scarves.

Large or small, morning, lunch-time or afternoon, there is only one way to wear your new spring hat: square on top of the head and tilted slightly forward.

Pre-view of Earls Court Fashions

A PRE-VIEW of fashions to be shown exclusively at the Ideal Home Exhibition in London next month was given to Press representatives in Birmingham this week when Brilkie, Ltd., included in their spring and summer fashion parade many of the items which will be on view at Earls Court.

Coinciding with the London parades, a miniature display will be staged in Birmingham, where identical models will be shown with the exhibition parades, thus giving Midland women an insight into a section of the exhibition in their home area.

The new season's range is bigger than ever, with a wider variety of materials and patterns, and despite increasing costs there are some remarkably good value dresses for as little as 27s. 6d.

Materials included a permanent seersucker, a rayon which had the appearance of shantung, crease-resisting poplin, rayon jersey, processed viole, iridescent jaspé resembling a tropical worsted, Bedford cord, and seersucker viole—the lightest form of seersucker made in this country.

WORLD DAY OF PRAYER SERVICE

TO-MORROW is Women's World Day of Prayer, celebrated annually on the first Friday in Lent.

This movement was started about 18 years ago by a small band of women of various denominations in London.

The late Miss Bertha Pick, a deacon of Queen's Road Baptist Church, Coventry, who was also a member of the Baptist Missionary Society, was asked to be responsible for the service each year in Coventry. This she did until her death in 1948. At the first service, the congregation numbered six, but last year over 250 women attended the service at St. Thomas's Church.

Since Miss Pick's death, a committee of Anglican and Free Church women have arranged the service alternately in Anglican and Nonconformist churches.

This year, the service will be held at Queen's Road Baptist Church, at 3 p.m., when Coventry women from 86 churches of various denominations will take part in a world-wide service of intercession with women of 93 countries.

Hospitality For Festival

COVENTRY Women's Voluntary Service is preparing a register of local people who are willing to extend private hospitality to visitors from abroad to the Festival of Britain.

Householders who are prepared to offer such accommodation should send details to the W.V.S. Headquarters, 90, Gosford Street, stating such items as the accommodation available and distance from the station.

A CENTURY OF FINE CARPETS ON SHOW

AN opportunity is afforded Coventry's home-lovers this week of being able to view some rare specimens of carpets made as long ago as 1851.

These carpets, which are museum pieces of well-known manufacturers in the country, are staged side by side with the most modern designs to form an 1851 to 1951 exhibition at Holbrooks, Ltd.

The exhibits, representative of the craftsmanship of a century ago, illustrate the wonderful depth of colour obtained by the use of vegetable dyes. Even at the age of 100 years, they show no sign of fading or discoloration, even though they have been subjected to strong light and sunshine.

LARGE SPECIMEN

The largest exhibit is a velvet pile Wilton, 17ft. 6ins. by 13ft. 6ins., of a hundred years ago. It is woven in two pieces — a feat in those days to weave such a width—and embodies all the old vegetable dyes used in that period. So great is the richness of colour obtained that the roses, which form only a fraction of an exquisite design, appear almost real.

Three uncut pile specimens were woven on a Jacquard handloom in 1850 for Balmoral Castle and a blue and gold lion and coronet design Brussels carpet woven on a power loom.

Two pieces were woven in 1866 for King Carol of Roumania—one a street scene showing a horse-drawn cab being driven along a cobbled street, and another on which were woven the heads of the royal family.

SYLVAN SCENE

An 1880 Brussels strip is of a particularly attractive sylvan scene with rippling stream and banks of natural looking vegetation.

It is clear from a glance at all these specimens that the craftsmen of a century ago were not subjected to anything like the pressure of time and change of fashion experienced in these days.

The exhibition is well worth a visit, for it emphasises the joys which must have been experienced when furnishing in days when such products of the old craftsmen were available.

EASY NEEDLE THREADING

THIS week's gadget news relates to a new sewing aid—an automatic needle threader which will be a boon to those women who just cannot find the eye.

All that is required is to drop a needle into the threader, eye down, hang the cotton over a hook, press a button and the needle is ready for use. Price 2s. from local drapers.

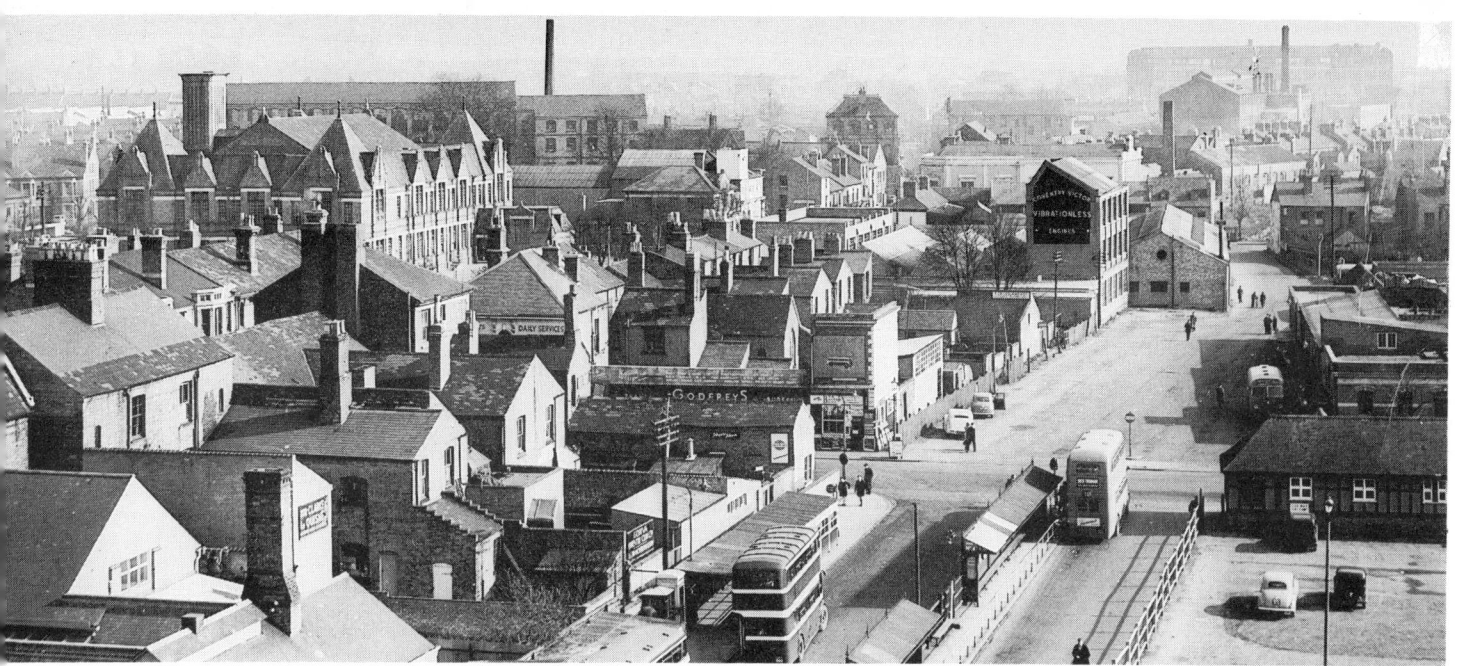

The view from the Fire Station Tower, March 1, 1951

King George VI and Queen Elizabeth visit the city,
February 5, 1951

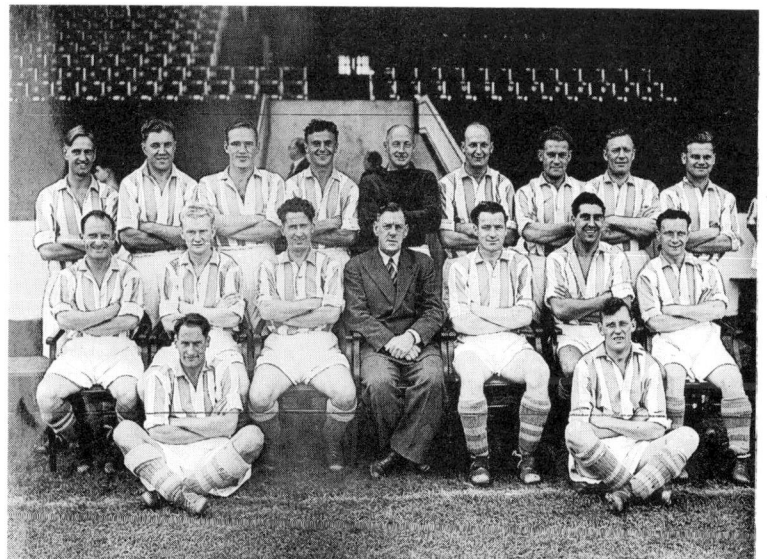

Coventry City F.C., August 1951

St John's, from Fleet Street, with Hill Street facing (right), 1952

THE NEW ERA

WITH the solemn obsequies which will to-day mark the passing of King George to his last resting place, this nation will come to what may be regarded by many as the end of a period in its long and glorious history and the beginning of a new era. Gone is a King who, despite physical handicaps, lived a good life and performed a heavy task bravely and well and upon his young daughter falls a burden whose weight will be hard to bear. But young as she is Queen Elizabeth is well-equipped, both by natural gifts and training, to carry out the duties that have been laid upon her.

GOLF TRIALS   15.2.52.

MUCH of the hope for the future prestige of Britain's women golfers lies in the hands of Pamela Davies, of Coventry, the most promising young woman golfer in the country. Only three years after beginning to play serious golf she has earned herself a place in the trials for Britain's Curtis Cup team.

While she was at school Pamela played golf at the Finham course in Coventry, but it was not until she left school in 1949 that she began to take the game seriously. Then, in her first big match, she won the Girls' Championship. Her consistent play won her a place in the Warwickshire team, and in 1950 she was a finalist in the Warwickshire, Midland Counties and English Women's Championships. She also played for England against Australia. Last year she represented England against Scotland, Wales and Ireland, and reached the quarter finals of the English Women's Championship.

Bishop Street, February 22, 1952

Market Square, February 29, 1952

Models:
14 h.p. SALOON
18 h.p. SALOON
2½ litre SPORTS

LEA-FRANCIS
LF
COVENTRY

Maker:
LEA-FRANCIS CARS LTD.
Much Park St.
COVENTRY

1952

THREE MODELS are featured in the current Lea-Francis range, two of which have a similar power unit, relatively minor modifications being made to increase the power output for the sports model. The design of the Lea-Francis engines is of particular interest in that the overhead valves are operated by twin camshafts carried high on each side of the cylinder block. One camshaft operates the inlet valves and the other the exhaust valves and the inlet and exhaust ports are served by almost straight passages in the head.

This system, which has been patented by Lea-Francis, offers numerous advantages—it enables the sparking plugs to be positioned between the valve ports, the whole of the cylinder head and valve gear can be removed in one simple operation and, with the short push rods, the weight of the valve gear is appreciably reduced so that wear is small and tappet adjustment is long lived due to the small degree of expansion of the short rods.

14 h.p. Saloon

Engine		
Cylinders	..	4
Capacity	..	1,767 c.c.
Bore	..	75 mm.
Stroke	..	100 mm.
Valves	..	Overhead
Compression Ratio	..	7.25:1
Max. B.H.P.	..	70 at 4,700 r.p.m.
R.A.C. Rating	..	13.9 h.p.
Transmission		
Clutch	..	Single dry plate
Gearbox	..	Four speeds fwd.
Control	..	Central Lever
Overall Ratios:		
Top	..	4.88
Third	..	6.90
Second	..	10.40
First	..	16.85
Rear Axle	..	Hypoid Bevel
Suspension		
Front	..	Independent. Torsion Bars
Rear	..	Semi-elliptic Leaf
Brakes	..	Hydraulic
Dimensions		
Wheelbase	..	9 ft. 3 ins.
Track	(front)	4 ft. 4½ ins.
	(rear)	4 ft. 4½ ins.
Overall Length	..	15 ft. 1 in.
Overall Width	..	5 ft. 4½ ins.
Overall Height	..	5 ft. 0½ in.
Tyre Size	..	6.00—16
Weight Dry	..	2,912 lb.
Fuel Tank Capacity	..	11 galls.
Price		
Model: Four-light Saloon		
Basic £1,130 plus P.T.		Total £1,759 5s. 6d.

14 h.p. Saloon

SEPTEMBER 10 1952

A MEETING between Midland M.P.s and trade unionists is being held to discuss the deterioration in employment in engineering.

Mr. J. L. (Jack) Jones, Coventry district secretary of the Confederation of Shipbuilding and Engineering Unions said today: "We are going to have in the next few months the biggest fight we have had for years to maintain employment in the motor industry.

"Competition is intense, particularly on the Continent in relation to cars and tractors."

Coventry To Have a Lord Mayor

The Queen has conferred a Lord Mayoralty on Coventry in commemoration of her Coronation.

News of the raising of the city's civic status is contained in a Home Office announcement issued to-day which states:

The Queen, on the recommendation of the Home Secretary, has been graciously pleased to command that in commemoration of Her Majesty's Coronation the chief magistrate, now and for the time being, of the city of Coventry, shall be styled Lord Mayor of Coventry.

1.6.53.

Coronation Ceremony of 1953

FROM OUR OWN REPORTER.
Westminster Abbey, June 2.

"RECEIVING the gleaming emblem from the Dean, the Primate held the great Crown of England above Her Majesty and reverently placed it upon her head. It was the thrilling, dramatic moment for which almost the whole world had been waiting. Within the Abbey the long silence ended. Fervent, exultant shouts of "God Save the Queen," resounded round the "Parish church of the Empire." Princes and princesses, peers and peeresses put on their coronets and caps, and the Kings - at - Arms, their crowns.

TRIUMPH FANFARE

The massed trumpeters played a triumphant fanfare, and the bells in the north-west tower clanged out the momentous tidings. Simultaneously, salutes were fired by the guns at the Tower of London, and in Hyde Park, and the waiting throngs outside the Abbey joined in the great acclamation with full throated shouts and cheers.

There was quiet in the church again as the Archbishop prayed: "God crown you with a crown of glory and righteousness, that having a right faith and manifold fruit of good works, you may obtain the crown of an everlasting kingdom by the gift of Him whose kingdom endureth for ever."

Much Park Street, c.1953

Market Street, with Woolworth's being built, 1953

Hunting for a bargain, Woolworth's, 1954

Demolition of the City Arcade is almost complete, July 1, 1954. Development of the Precinct, Market Street North and the site around is about to begin

GREAT PROGRESS IN RECONSTRUCTION

AT the end of a year of great achievement in the civic sphere Coventry can look forward to 1954 as "a Leap Year for planning." The words are those of Alderman G. E. Hodgkinson, chairman of the Planning and Redevelopment Committee.

Of the coming year he told "The Coventry Evening Telegraph": All the conditions are there for rapid progress as a result of the relaxing of licensing restrictions and regulations governing capital allocations for blitzed cities.

"The availability of materials and manpower are now the main factors controlling the speed and tempo of central redevelopment."

Alderman Hodgkinson added that he would like to see a speed-up of compulsory purchase procedure and an early declaration on the city's re-development plan which was subject to inquiry early in 1953.

"We are concerned with the overall picture of the city in respect of war damage and blighted areas which need comprehensive treatment," he said.

Progress in 1953

Ever since the war Coventry's proposed new city centre has been a local and national talking point. Overseas journals have devoted columns to the plans for a new Coventry centre rising on the ruins of the buildings destroyed in the air raids.

So much planned, so much written, and so little to show for it until 1953.

Suddenly the whole project has blazed into life with an incessant and exciting clatter of excavators and mammoth cranes. Bit by bit the public have seen the pieces fit-

ting snugly into the jigsaw of future Coventry.

In the words of Alderman Hodgkinson, chairman of the Planning and Redevelopment Committee: "One of the most exciting things in Coventry's municipal life to-day. . . ."

Shops and Stores

A year of real progress in central redevelopment has seen the official opening by Lord Silkin of Broadgate House, the first block to be completed.

Shopping facilities have received a boost in the summer opening of the first instalment of Woolworth's store.

A start, and substantial progress, has been made on the Marks and Spencer store. Another, that of Owen Owen, has risen floor by floor to dominate the Burges end of the city centre.

Latterly, contractors have begun operations on the site for the new hotel, adjacent to the Owen Owen project.

Civic Buildings

Within a stone's throw of all the obvious activity that captures public interest, builders have been busy on such enterprises as the College of Art and Technology in Cope Street, the new Council offices in Earl Street, and site preparation for a diversionary road in Little Park Street, in readiness for the new police headquarters.

Still further afield, the steel framework for the municipal bus transport garage in Sandy Lane has been erected, and at Barras Heath a beginning has been made on the site for the new wholesale market.

IN DEMAND

"I hope you will be able to give me a rise, sir, as three other companies are after me."

"Really?"

"Yes, sir—the gas company, the electricity company, and the furniture company."

22.12.53

First Part of Marks & Spencer Block to be Opened at Easter

ANOTHER big step forward in the provision of new shopping facilities in the centre of Coventry will be taken at Easter, when part of the Marks and Spencer store in the Precinct is opened.

The new Owen Owen store progresses, January 12, 1954

The Lord Mayor, Ald. John Fennell, opens the Owen Owen store, October 1, 1954

The Precinct's new bridge under construction, May 24, 1955

Work goes on in the Precinct, 1955

Annual Review of St John Ambulance Brigade, Humber Road, Stoke, c.1955

Hertford Street, August 1, 1955

Luxury at the Leofric

1955

THE CARPET — all five miles of it — was spread out for the opening of Britain's first new post-war hotel on April 28, 1955.

It was Coventry's Leofric Hotel, built at a cost of £800,000, with 108 luxury bedrooms, each wired for TV, and with 3,500 electric points.

The hotel, so we were told, was equipped with 16 tons of china, 15,000 knives, forks and spoons, 1,325 chairs and 1,000 each of table cloths, sheets and towels.

The man behind the new structure was 72-year-old Mr. Willie Watson, building manager for Sir Robert McAlpine and Sons Ltd.

Ironmonger Row dual-carriageway awaits its final surface, August 24, 1955

23.11.55.

The Eaton Road "bulge" in Coventry, is now taking shape The road has been made a one-way thoroughfare. The work is part of the traffic lights scheme for the five-ways crossing at Greyfriars Green. This picture was taken from Warwick Road to-day.

WITH improved weather and the delivery of materials, work has been resumed on the construction of this bridge at the rear of Coventry Council House. It will link the Council House with St. Mary's Hall. Accommodation will be provided in the hall for various civic engagements, to relieve congestion in the Council House. 16.3.56.

What kind of shows did viewers see in those salad days of 14in. screens and black and white ITV in the Midlands?

MONDAYS put the accent on drama, presenting "International Theatre" with 90-minute plays. In contrast there was a panel game called "What's It All About?"

TUESDAYS set a new vogue for the kids — and their dads — with the first of a popular series. It was back to the days of Sherwood Forest with Richard Greene starring in "The Adventures of Robin Hood."

Then there was a local quiz show with cash prizes called "Hit the Limit" and a George and Alfred Black variety show, "Strike a New Note."

WEDNESDAYS saw Hughie Green in his quiz "Double Your Money," an hour long spectacle featuring on alternate weeks, Mantovani and his Orchestra and Vera Lynn.

Then came the first of twice-a-week screenings of "I Love Lucy" starring Lucille Ball and her then husband Desi Arnaz.

It was decided to double up on the Lucy shows so that we in the Midlands could catch up on the series already seen in the London area.

THURSDAYS brought us Liberace, complete with candelabra and piano in "a comedy hour of music, dancing and laughter." It also brought us "Meet the Professor," a weekly popular science magazine with questions posed by an imaginary West Bromwich family called Bones.

FRIDAYS had "Take Your Pick" with Michael Miles followed by a programme that, like Robin Hood, became something of a cult.

It was the American crime series, "Dragnet" starring Jack Webb of the staccato voice and dead-pan face as Sgt. Joe Friday.

Couldn't very well put him on any other night, could they?

SATURDAYS gave us "Hometown Saturday Night," a variety programme with local artists and personalities relayed from halls in Midlands towns.

Waving the baton and keeping us in the mood was bandleader Joe Loss.

SUNDAYS — and of course, "Sunday Night at the Palladium," rated the top show of the week. There was the second "I Love Lucy," and a show all about pop music and recording stars presented by Jack Jackson.

Awaiting the arrival of the Queen, March 23, 1956

74

New Jaguar engines are run for the first time, March 1956

Enthronement of the Rt Rev Cuthbert Bardsley as Bishop of Coventry, May 7, 1956

St John's, Corporation Street/Hill Street, May 11, 1957. The large building (top left) is the old Rudge Whitworth works in Spon Street

Little Park Street, April 27, 1957

The site of the Coventry Evening Telegraph building, Corporation Street, May 1, 1957

The Coventry
Evening Telegraph

No. 20,546 [67th Year]. THURSDAY, MAY 23, 1957. 2½d.

St. Mary's Hall Ceremony Makes TV History
COVENTRY'S FIRST WOMAN LORD MAYOR

Mrs. P. M. Hyde Pledges 'Dignity and Humility'

THOUSANDS of television viewers in the Midlands and the North to-day watched the installation of Mrs. P. M. Hyde as new Lord Mayor of Coventry.

It was a doubly historic occasion — the first time the city has had a woman Lord Mayor and the first time a mayor-making ceremony anywhere has been televised.

Reception of the programme, which lasted 90 minutes, was good. Elderly people in Walsgrave and Wyken watched the installation of Mrs. Alderman Hyde—president of their Old Age Pensioners' association branches—on television at Wyken Working Men's Club and Walsgrave Baptist Chapel.

Before she became an alderman, Mrs. Hyde represented Walsgrave Ward on the City Council.

COLOURFUL

Assembled in the hall under the glare of floodlighting installed for the cameras, the robed aldermen and councillors made a colourful gathering.

The proceedings were watched by about 220 people in the body of the hall, among them nine years old Terence, grandson of the new Lord Mayor, and other members of the family.

In a speech of thanks Mrs. Hyde said: "I hope to fulfil this office with the dignity it ought to have and a humility and friendliness to all people, irrespective of their colour and creed.

WELCOME

"Let them come to the Lord Mayor's office knowing that there is a warmth of welcome in my heart and in that of the City Council."

The resolution of election of Mrs. Hyde to the office of Lord (Continued on Page 9.)

No Film on ATV News

PLANS had been made to film part of the ceremony for inclusion in the ATV Midland News this evening, but the cameraman's transport broke down on the way to Coventry.

Efforts to get the vehicle working in time to arrive at St. Mary's Hall before the end of the Mayor-making were of no avail.

Civic Theatre Management

AFTER the mayor-making ceremony in St. Mary's Hall to-day, the formal business of the annual meeting of Coventry City Council was carried out.

This included the selection of ten Council members to subscribe to the Memorandum of the Association of the Belgrade Theatre Trust (Coventry) Ltd., and to serve on the Council of Management for 1957-58.

They were Alderman S. Stringer (chairman); Mrs. Alderman E. A. Allen, Alderman W. H. Edwards, Councillors J. D. Berry, W. R. Jones, G. S. N. Richards, E. A. C. Roberts, E. M. Rogers, F. Walsh, and A. J. Waugh.

The five non-council members nominated were Mr. Leonard Turner, Mr. Launcelot Wheatley, Miss N. Casson, Mr. W. Wilson, Mr. R. B. Mather.

TV cameras capture the scene in St. Mary's Hall as Mrs Alderman P. M. Hyde makes her first speech as the new Lord Mayor of Coventry. (More pictures on Pages 10, 11 and 13.)

ENGINEERS TAKE THE 'STRINGS' RISE

THE engineering unions to-day accepted the employers' offer of pay increases of 9s. to 11s. a week — with the "strings" including a year's standstill in demands.

The increases date from Monday next.

The drawn-out dispute over the claim for a 10 per cent. increase for 2,500,000 engineering workers was settled at a London meeting between representatives of the Confederation of Shipbuilding and Engineering Unions and the Engineering and Allied Employers' National Federation.

Wages Grades

Mr. W. J. Carron, president of the Amalgamated Engineering Union, said after the meeting: "We hope that as a result of the settlement our industry will benefit."

The increases will be added to the consolidated rates for timeworkers and in the case of workers paid by results it will be added to existing supplements.

Commenting on the £70 million estimate, Mr. F. C. Braby, the Employers' president, said: "That is a very large sum and some firms have not yet been able to recover from last year's settlement. This is going to make things

Foot-and-Mouth

An outbreak of foot and mouth disease was confirmed in Jersey to-day and the whole island was declared a restricted area. Six cows, six heifers, three sows and 20 young pigs were destroyed.

Attitude Vindicated
Says Mr. Urwin

COMMENTING on the wages settlement, Mr. Harry Urwin, Coventry district secretary of the Confederation of Shipbuilding and Engineering Unions, said: "Everybody will be pleased that a wages agreement has now been reached after discussions which have been dragging on since last September.

"It means that the unions' attitude has been vindicated. There will, however, be apprehension felt by some members concerning the conditions that have been attached."

extremely difficult for some firms who are unable to raise their prices."

Mr. Braby explained that the proposal in the Court of Inquiry report that a national joint council should be set up for the industry would be considered by both sides at a later date.

Dartmoor Man:

Police kept watch on the Gravesend-Tilbury ferry to-day in the hunt for William Fowler, the Dartmoor prisoner who escaped.

It is believed that he has previously used the ferry in his bid to find a ship bound for the Continent.

WHAT THE VIEWERS SAW

A television close-up of Mrs. Hyde. She is being congratulated by her predecessor, Alderman W. I. Thomson.

Lord Salisbury on 'Most Important' Suez Decision

THE Marquess of Salisbury, who recently resigned as Lord President of the Council over the recall of Archbishop Makarios, drawing attention in the Lords to-day to the Government's statement on the Suez Canal, said:

"This decision to accept Nasser's terms, whether in protest or not, whether as a temporary arrangement or as a final settlement, seems to be, let us face the fact, a decision of the most important kind which may have the most far-reaching repercussions."

Lord Salisbury said our intervention had brought the United States into the Middle East. "We can register some satisfaction at being a by-product of our policy which I am sure we are all glad to welcome."

Lord Salisbury said that prac-

tical and businesslike as the Prime Minister's speech had been, he could not help asking himself whether a practical approach was all that was required in circumstances like these when the whole principle of international good faith on which civilisation itself rested was in jeopardy.

12 Servicemen in Crashed Plane

A French Privateer aircraft with about 12 Servicemen on board crashed last night on a plateau near Biskra, Eastern Algeria, it was learned in Paris to-day.

Reports said there were few survivors. The aircraft was from the Fleet Air Arm base at Karouba, Northern Tunisia.

ALREADY nearly 40ft. above the ground, the zig-zag walls of the new Coventry Cathedral still have a long way to rise.
When the great building is completed in five years' time, they will be about 88ft. high—as high as the point marked on the old Cathedral tower in this latest photograph of the site.

In this view from the north-east, the shape of the new Cathedral can be seen behind a web of scaffolding. On the right is Holy Trinity Church and, neighbouring the site, the Georgian house in Priory Row, now used as offices.

In the near left-hand corner of the photograph is the cirular base of the Guild Chapel, with the link which attaches it to the main building.

The nave level of the Cathedral is roughly at the present height of the link, about 20ft. above ground level at this point.

The Duchess of Kent (centre) with the Lord Mayor, Ald. Mrs Pearl Hyde, at the opening of the Belgrade Theatre, March 27, 1958

Coventry Carnival, c.1958

Jordan Well, January 9, 1959

The Reporters' Room, Coventry Evening Telegraph, 1959

West Orchard, September 1, 1959

*The Lord Mayor, Ald. W. H. Edwards, opens the first
part of the £3,000,000 inner ring road, December 23,
1959. The section, from London Road to St. Patrick's
Road, was completed in 5½ months*

Coventry Railway Station, February 12, 1960

Shirley Bassey

The King of the Diddymen, Ken Dodd

PROGRAMME

1. **OVERTURE**
   " Strike Up The Band " .... *Gershwin (arr. Pullon)*

2. **" SPRING IS IN THE AIR "**
   THE SIX DEBONAIRES
   introduce
   A Shower of Lovelies .... THE DEBUTANTES
   The Pitter Patter of .... **THE RAINDROPS**
   On a Zephyr Breeze .... **FREDDIE SALES**
   Those April Fools .... **THE THREE MONARCHS**
   The Pipes of Pan .... **KEN DODD**

   And that Sophisticated Touch of Spring
   SHIRLEY BASSEY

3. **KEN DODD**
   Starts the Fun

4. **LES MATHURINS**
   Cascadeurs Burlesques

5. **FREDDIE SALES**
   " Baby Talk "

6. **THE RAINDROPS**
   T.V.'s Brightest and Newest Vocal Group

7. **" LIGHT AS A FEATHER "**
   THE DEBUTANTES
   and
   THE SIX DEBONAIRES

8. **KEN DODD**
   The Unpredictable

9. **" FIESTA IN CUBA "**   April 1960
   The Revellers :
   THE SIX DEBONAIRES   THE DEBUTANTES

   The Star of the Night :
   SHIRLEY BASSEY

10. *INTERVAL (15 minutes)*

11. **" DON'T YOU AGREE?"**
    with THE SIX DEBONAIRES
    who introduce
    THE 16 DEBUTANTES

12. **LES FRANK MEDINI**
    Sensational New Continental Speciality

13. **" NOW IT CAN BE TOLD "**
    Brunhilde .... BERYL BOLTON
    German Commandant .... TREVOR GRIFFITHS
    Old Man .... BILL RICHARDS
    Humphrey .... **FREDDIE SALES**
    Anthony .... PAUL MEAD

14. **THREE MONARCHS**
    Those Crazy Harmonica Wizards

15. **KEN DODD**
    Still Unpredictable

16. The Fabulous
    SHIRLEY BASSEY

17. **FINALE**
    The Entire Company says Farewell

PROGRAMME CONTINUED OVERL

Properties in New Buildings, due for demolition, August, 1960

The first Coventry-to-London motorway express coach, operated by the Midland Red, leaves Pool Meadow, September 1, 1960

5.9.60.

The quiet strike is over

THE "silent strikers" of Coventry Colliery were back at work today.

The West Midlands Division of the National Coal Board and the Warwickshire District of the National Union of Mineworkers, have said they had no information about the absence at Keresley last week of about 130 day-shift and 150 night-shift workers.

The men's absence is believed to be connected with a grievance about the make-up of their pay.

They stayed away from work towards the end of last week after staging a "go slow."

Two houses struck by lightning

TWO houses in Anchorway Road, Coventry, were struck by lightning during the week-end.

In one house were Mr. and Mrs. R. Beaufoy, their three sons, and Mr. Beaufoy's 65-year-old mother. In the other were Mr. and Mrs. H. Rose. The beams of both houses caught fire and firemen had to strip part of both roofs.

Mrs. Rose said: "I saw the reflection of a huge ball of fire reflected in the window of the houses opposite. Then there was a terrific crash."

Hertford Street, February 17, 1961

83

Sovereign Place, The Butts, February 2, 1961

Hillfields, May 10, 1961

The Armstrong Whitworth Aircraft works, Baginton, May 18, 1961

Armstrong Whitworth Argosy, the last of their Coventry-built aircraft, 1961

Opera House, Hales Street, July 21, 1961

Upper Well Street, November 24, 1961

Spon End flats continue to grow, August 18, 1961

Jordan Well, October 23, 1961

The Coventry Evening Telegraph

LAST EDITION

No. 22,070 [72nd Year]　　　FRIDAY, MAY 25, 1962　　　* * *　　　2¼d.

Coventry Gives Enthusiastic Welcome to Royal Visitors

QUEEN AT CONSECRATION SERVICE IN CATHEDRAL

Climax of a Great Day

IN the presence of the Queen, Princess Margaret and the Earl of Snowdon the new Coventry Cathedral was Consecrated today by the Bishop, Dr. Cuthbert Bardsley.

After the Consecration ceremony a packed congregation of about 2,000 — together with millions watching it on television — heard the Archbishop of Canterbury, Dr. A. M. Ramsey, describe the new St. Michael's as "a house in which all the arts and the craftsmanship of our time have united — stone, wood, glass, metal; the designer, the builder, the painter, the sculptor."

"A generation has made its offering of beauty in the service of God," Dr. Ramsey continued. "It is the people's Cathedral, your Cathedral, linking Church and people together.

"Here, too, is a house which speaks of peace, of reconciliation. Nations which have been divided see in it a sign that God can forgive, can unite, God can make men brothers.

"It is a prophecy, for as a new Cathedral rises from the ashes, so a new world of partnership and brotherhood can, by God's goodness, rise from the miseries of the past."

COUNCIL PRESENTED

The Consecration Service — an occasion of pageantry, beauty and moving dedication — was the greatest event in what many will remember as Coventry' greatest day.

From early morning crowds gathered in the decorated streets. They gave the royal visitors an enthusiastic welcome as they drove from Coventry Station through the city centre to the Council House.

There a note of simplicity crept into the programme as the Lord Mayor, Alderman A. J. Waugh, presented members of the City Council to the Queen.

Recognising Alderman G. E. Hodgkinson, whom she has met on previous visits, the Queen greeted him with the message: "Nice to be back."

Tour of New Station

The Queen attended a celebration luncheon in St. Mary's Hall while Princess Margaret and Lord Snowdon joined another gathering at the Hotel Leofric Afterwards, when they returned to the royal train to prepare for the Consecration Sevice, they all took the opportunity to tour the new railway station.

Broadgate was even more crowded when the royal party returned on their way to the Cathedral. They passed through Trinity Churchyard to the West Gate of the old Cathedral, and then walked through the ruins.

The Queen was welcomed by the Bishop and by the Provost, the Very Rev. H. C. N. Williams, who presented to her the architect, Sir Basil Spence, and the leading officials responsible for the Cathedral's reconstruction.

THE Provost, the Very Rev. H. C. N. Williams, leads the Queen through the ruins of the old Cathedral for the consecration service in the new. They are followed by the Bishop of Coventry, Dr. Cuthbert Bardsley, accompanying Princess Margaret and Lord Snowdon. In front is the Provost's Verger, Mr. John Wickens. The television monitors enabled the guests in the ruins to follow the service in the Cathedral. This was the last procession to enter the Cathedral before the entry of the Bishop of Coventry to conduct the service.

87

The Queen signing the distinguished visitors' book at the Council House today, watched by the Lord Mayor. In the background are Princess Margaret and the Earl of Snowdon. 25.5.62

Famous racing driver, Donald Cambell, with his Bluebird car at Motor Panels, October 31, 1962

For lively comment on the world of Theatre

Read . . .

The Coventry
Evening Telegraph

Instructress Dorothy Seaton at Livingstone Road Baths, May 1962

Girls from Barkers' Butts Secondary Modern School enjoy the wintry sunshine on the frozen pool in Naul's Mill Park, January 12, 1963. Hockey had been cancelled because of the state of the pitches

Cheylesmore shops, March 1, 1963

Coventry Carnival, June 15, 1963

Beauty queens take part in an in-store promotion, c.1963

● Still celebrating . . . Directors, players and their wives of Third Division champions Coventry City were invited to the Coventry Theatre to watch the Spring Show and then to attend a reception with some of the stars. Here Manager Jimmy Hill, in the foreground with Jimmy Clitheroe, acknowledges a toast to his team given by Mr. S. H. Newsome (left), Managing Director of the theatre. Others in the picture, from left to right, are comedian Dickie Henderson, Susan Lane, Coventry City skipper George Curtis, comedian Jimmy Tarbuck and Mr. Derrick Robins, Chairman of Coventry City. 23.5.64

Pattison's Restaurant, Hertford Street, July 17, 1964

Part of the Courtelle section of the acetate and synthetics laboratory at Courtaulds Ltd., Lockhurst Lane, November 14, 1964

5.4.65.

PAYMENT books and forms for Coventry's rates-by-instalments plan, which starts on October 1, will begin to go out next week to the first of the 18,400 ratepayers who have opted to join the scheme.

The Council House computer is calculating the amounts due in monthly instalments from each ratepayer, and these will be printed on tear-off slips in paying-in books.

A BAND of nearly 80 elderly gentlemen met in the centre of Coventry today to remember an occasion half a century ago.

On August 6, 1914, the first of them some aged only 15, landed in France. They were the light-hearted flower of Britain's "contemptible little army," as the Kaiser termed it.

In the next four months they and their comrades, who lie in Flanders fields, earned undying fame as they fell in swathes during bitter battles.

Two Herald bugles are presented to the 13th Coventry Scout Band, prior to their making history by becoming the first Scout musicians to play in Westminster Abbey, January 11, 1966

Dedication of Eastern Green C. of E. School by the Bishop of Coventry, February 10, 1966

The Duke of Edinburgh in No 1 Heavy Machines Shop, Coventry Climax, June 22, 1966

Barr's Hill School Speech Day, Central Hall, October 20, 1966

94

Westwood C. of E. Primary School, December 16, 1966

Royal Show, July 7, 1967

The Lord Mayor, Ald. E. J. Williams, demonstrates the art of carol singing to boys from Caludon Castle and Woodlands schools, as they set off, with the aid of the Fire Brigade, December 15, 1967

Members of the Bees Speedway Team, March 27, 1968

Service No.	1967 Bus Routes
1	STOKE HEATH—Gosford Green—COUNCIL HOUSE—Hearsall Common—CHAPELFIELDS (Maudslay Hotel)
2	RADFORD (June Catesby Rd. & Burnaby Rd.)—Cheveral Avenue—Sandy Lane—BROADGATE—CHEYLESMORE (Daventry Buildings)
3	STOKE ALDERMOOR (Round House Road)—GAUMONT—Courtaulds—Lockhurst Lane—HEN LANE or HOLBROOKS
5	COUNDON (Norman Place Rd.)—Barkers Butts Lane—Hill Street—HIPPODROME (Hales Street)
6	POOL MEADOW—Gosford Green—WYKEN—WALSGRAVE (Projected alternately every 30 min. from Walsgrave via Bell Green to Aldermans Green or via Lentons Lane to the same point)
7	SEWALL HIGHWAY—Gosford Green—FORD ST. or HIPPODROME—Holyhead Road—Allesley—BROWN'S LANE (Daimler No. 2 Factory)
8	TILE HILL—Tile Hill Lane—Hearsall Common—Spon St.—POOL MEADOW (Additional buses every 15 min between JUNC BEECH BEECH TREE AVENUE/TILE HILL LANE and POOL MEADOW)
9	EARLSDON—Technical College—BROADGATE—Paynes Lane—COPSEWOOD (Bromleigh Drive)
10	BROWNSHILL GREEN—Browns Lane—Allesley—Allesley Old Rd.—Spon St.—CORPORATION ST.
11	GLENDOWER AVENUE—Allesley Old Rd.—Spon St.—Smithford St.—COUNCIL HOUSE—Gosford Green—Copsewood—BINLEY
13	BROAD LANE—Hearsall Common—Technical College—CORPORATION ST.—Pool Meadow/Ford St.—London Rd.—BAGINTON AIRPORT or RYTON (Rootes)
14	INNER CIRCLE from Coventry Station via Queen Victoria Road, Holyhead Road, Radford, Sandy Lane, Foleshill Rd., Harnall Lane East, Swan Lane, Gosford Green, Gulson Rd., Parkside to Station
16 & 16A	KERESLEY VILLAGE—SHEPHERD & SHEPHERDESS (Keresley Rd.)—Radford Road—BROADGATE—Memorial Park—GREEN LANE (Crossway Rd) Certain buses diverted to Keresley Hospital instead of Keresley Village
17	BAGINTON (Oak)—Baginton Rd.—Leamington Rd.—BROADGATE
18	BURTON GREEN—Westwood Heath—Canley—Hearsall Common—Technical College—Queen Victoria Rd.—Corporation St.—POOL MEADOW
18A	CANLEY (Mitchell Avenue)—Burnsail Rd.—Hearsall Common—Spon St.—CORPORATION ST.
19	BERKSWELL (The Bear)—Eastern Green—Broad Lane—Hearsall Common, then as service 18
20	BEDWORTH—LONGFORD—Foleshill—Foleshill Rd.—BROADGATE—COVENTRY STATION
21	BELL GREEN—Courthouse Green—Stoney Stanton Rd.—BROADGATE—COVENTRY STATION

Lower Ford Street, November 12, 1969

COVENTRY INNER RING ROAD
COMPLETION OF DELIVERY
LAST OF 1476 BEAMS
SUPPLIED TO MESSRS. **GALLIFORD & SONS LTD., BY DOW MAC LTD.**

Celebrations as the last concrete beam is lowered into position on stage five of the ring road, August 28, 1969

The Brook Street (front), Berry Street (left) and Vernon Street "triangle," July 29, 1970

Flooding at Spon End, August 22, 1970

Primrose Hill Street, September 1, 1971

Princess Margaret talks to actress Glenda Jackson after a charity concert in Coventry Cathedral, November 18, 1972

CITY FREEMEN SUPPORT GREYFRIARS GREEN PLANS

15/4/72

PLANS for the future Greyfriars Green, as it will appear when the ring road is completed, received the support of Coventry Freemen's trustees when they saw them at the City Architect's Department yesterday afternoon.

Details were given by Mr. Terence Gregory, City Architect, and Mr. W. Shirran, Parks Director.

The green will be twice its present size when the inner ring road has been completed. It will have about 80 more trees than it had before the road scheme, and will be extended over part of Warwick Road to near Parkside Garage.

OFFICIAL OPENING
of
HEREWARD COLLEGE
on
2nd March 1972

Instructor Gil Robottom shows Jaguar apprentices Les Thompson and Andy Davies the art of restoration, with an 1896 Shand Mason horizontal static fire pump, 1973

100

Triumph's carworkers about to vote overwhelmingly in favour of a secret ballot on a proposed new flat-rate wages plan, August 27, 1973

Massey-Ferguson "milestone," January 23, 1974

C Shop, Herbert Machine Tools Ltd, Red Lane, June 1974

The City Fathers beam down on the six semi-finalists in the Carnival Queen contest, March 13, 1974

29.8.74.

RECORDS SET AS NURSES QUALIFY

RECORDS were set at the presentation of awards to nurses qualifying from the Coventry Orthopaedic Nursing School last night.

Not only was the 100 per cent. pass rate for the school maintained for the fifth year running, but 29 successful nurses made a record total.

The awards were made by Mr. R. James, consultant orthopaedic surgeon.

He said the Coventry and Warwickshire Hospital had been described as having a family atmosphere.

The launch of HMS Coventry, June 22, 1974

Singer Anita Harris leaves Walsgrave Hospital with her husband, Mike Margoli after treatment, July 10, 1976

1976

THE GREEN
PHARMACEUTICAL GROUP of COMPANIES

FOR SPECIALIST SERVICES
THROUGHOUT THE CITY OF COVENTRY

★
GREEN'S CAMERA
SPECIALISTS
22, MARKET WAY
Devoted to SERVICE and
Professional Advice upon
all aspects of photography

GREEN'S BEAUTY SHOP

1 Shelton Square
for all High Class Agency Cosmetics
... Gifts and Pharmacy requirements

GREEN'S PHARMACY
HERTFORD STREET
Offers comprehensive pharmaceutical service
until 7 p.m. 24-hour Electric Shaver
Repair and Sales Centre.

Branches at: **36 Heath Crescent.**
Green's Pharmacy, The Green, Meriden.
Solihull Pharmacy Ltd., Drury Lane, Solihull.
Green's Pharmacy, Station Road, Balsall Common.
Green's Pharmacy, Earlsdon Street, Coventry.

The Parish Church
of the Holy Trinity Coventry

The
Opening and Dedication
of the
Church Centre
(formerly HOLY TRINITY OLD NATIONAL SCHOOL)

by
THE LORD BISHOP OF COVENTRY
The Right Reverend Cuthbert K. N. Bardsley, C.B.E., D.D.

SATURDAY 6th SEPTEMBER 1975
3 p.m.

Part of the Owen Owen queue for the Sale, July 24, 1976

4,000 at St George's Day parades

NUMBERS at St George's Day Scout parades in Coventry have grown so large that an extra church had to be used for yesterday's services.

Normally the Scouts use the Cathedral and Holy Trinity Church. But so many parents and friends could not find seats.

So yesterday the Methodist Central Hall was also brought into use. Even then all three churches were filled with Scouts, Guides, Cubs, Brownies and their parents, friends and relatives.

Mr Norman Heggrity, an assistant commissioner for Coventry Scouts, said that 2,570 Scouts had been joined by 1,400 guests.

25. 4. 77

The Queen's Silver Jubilee

1952 1977

May this old land revive and be
Again a star set in the sea.
A Kingdom fit for such as She
With glories yet undreamt.
JOHN MASEFIELD

A party to celebrate the Queen's Silver Jubilee, Byfield Road, Coundon, June 6, 1977

Their pile of pennies claimed as record

A NEW WORLD record for a pile of pennies has been claimed by a Coundon public house in Coventry.

Landlord Mr. Mick Keane is hoping that the achievement by his customers will restore the pub's name in the Guinness Book of records for next year.

A giant column of 2p coins was pushed over by Coventry City soccer skipper Terry Yorath and the one-hour counting operation by bank cashiers showed the total to be £2,053.24.

9.11.78.

PAT JENKS is setting off on a 13½-mile walk that ties in with a world wide event.

Pat from Keresley Road, Coventry will be walking from Meriden to Keresley calling in for refreshment at Women's Institutes on the way.

She'll be carrying a replica flag from institute to institute, which will eventually tour Britain and later be taken overseas to Germany.

Fund

And her walk will be copied by women all over the world.

The event is in aid of the Associated Country Women of the World, which has eight million members in 67 countries. It strives to build international friendship and understanding among women and seeks to improve rural conditions.

Being a member of a Women's Institute means that you automatically belong to ACWW.

Funds come from a "penny for friendship" scheme, when each member is asked every year to give a small sum. Projects exist to help malnourished children, to ban war toys and to encourage parental love, even in our Western countries.

2.8.79.

An unusual attraction in carnival week, this Royal Navy Search and Rescue helicopter certainly intrigued visitors to the Precinct, June 6, 1978

Blood donors receiving awards for having given 50 pints of blood. The Lord Mayor, Coun. Ralph Clews, makes the presentations, March 7, 1978

HOLY Trinity Church, Coventry, was packed yesterday for a special service to commemorate the 60th anniversary of the Royal Air Force.

The service followed a parade of about 400 people from Coventry Police headquarters in Little Park Street.

Group Captain the Reverend Tom Knight, now rector of Southam and a former commanding officer of RAF Gaydon, was guest preacher at the service.

A salute was taken on the Broadgate island by Councillor Ken Benfield.

The parade was led by the band of the Air Training Corps from Leamington. Squadron Leader John Ward, Birmingham and Warwickshire Wing Officer of the Air Training Corps, was the parade marshal.

It included contingents of the Royal Air Forces Association, the Polish Association, the RAFA Hinckley and Rugby branch, the Airborne Forces Association, the Parachute Regiment, the Burma Star Association, the Dunkirk Veterans Association, the Royal British Legion, the Royal Artillery Association, and the Royal Naval Association. 3.4.78

THERE'S a special end-of-term feeling at Earlsdon junior girls' school, Coventry. When the 237 children depart for the summer holidays, the doors close on single-sex state primary education in the city 8.7.78.

A REAL HISTORY LESSON

By DAVID BRINDLE

TUNING in as radio history was made in Coventry today were pupils of Walsgrave Junior School.

Two dozen children in Class 1 were up bright and early to greet the new local radio station for Coventry and Warwickshire, Mercia Sound.

As the station went on the air for the first time at 6.58 a.m., the youngsters were already at their desks.

Overture

Later, as they prepared their own breakfasts in the school kitchen, their message to the Mercia Sound team was broadcast on the first show, presented by Gordon Astley.

"It was the children's own idea to make it a special occasion," said their teacher, Mrs Vi Hemmings. "They felt that it was living history."

Early class as Mercia Sound goes on the air

Without fuss or ceremony, Mercia Sound began broadcasting 19 hours a day of music, news and sport from Hertford Place, Coventry.

After a brief overture, there was the simple announcement: "This is Mercia Sound on 220 metres medium wave, 1359 kHz and 95.9 VHF stereo. For the very first time, good morning from Mercia Sound."

There was then a jingle, followed by the 7 a.m. national and local news bulletins and, at 7.05, the Gordon Astley show. His first record was "This is it" by Dan Hartman.

Britain's 21st independent local radio station has been set up at a cost of £350,000 by Midland Community Radio Ltd. Its programme plans were published today.

The company say that music will predominate at first but that there will be a gradual move towards an equal division between music and other items. They say: "We reject the concept of being a juke box of the air."

24-hour hope

Also promised in the long term are children's and women's programmes, a regular feature on community schools in Coventry and Warwickshire, and educational features.

The chairman of Midland Community Radio, Mr John Butterworth, said that they hoped to move towards 24-hour broadcasting to cater for shift workers.

23.5.80.

Kicking off . . . disc jockey Gordon Astley, whose first record was "This is it."

Bablake School CC take school cricket's top honours in the area, July 26, 1980

Sports go-ahead

Plans to turn Coventry Park Zoo into a sports centre have been approved by West Midland planners.

Mr. Alfred Wood the county planner, said in a report to the planning committee yesterday, that the zoo had been "something of a failure," while a sports centre would be more of an asset to the local community.

The scheme, put forward by Miereel Ltd. involved the construction of six indoor and four outdoor tennis courts, six badminton courts and eight squash courts, toegether with a clubhouse and car park on a five-acre site.

17 JUL 1980

The committee also gave approval to plans for a motor cycle museum on the site of the Oaktree Cafe on Coventry Road, Bickenhill.

That sound again
1980

ONE grim reminder of the Blitz will be the sounding of sirens and alarm bells in the city centre at 7 p.m. on Friday.

It will mark the start of a "Fire Watch," 40 years to the minute after the alarms sounded on November 14, 1940.

Taking part are members of the city's Junior Chamber of Commerce who will tour areas of the city which suffered destruction in the raid.

B.L. Heritage Collection showroom, August 19, 1980

Telegraph beauty contest finalists, March 30, 1981

31.12.81.

Borg approves £2m Coventry tennis move

Coventry's new £2m tennis centre has received the Bjorn Borg stamp of approval.

After the opening of Grand Prix Racquet Centre, the former Wimbledon champion said: "This club is exactly what you need in England and the very best thing for the development of the game."

The eight indoor courts boast a surface similar to the one on which Borg learned the skills which enabled him to dominate world tennis for five years.

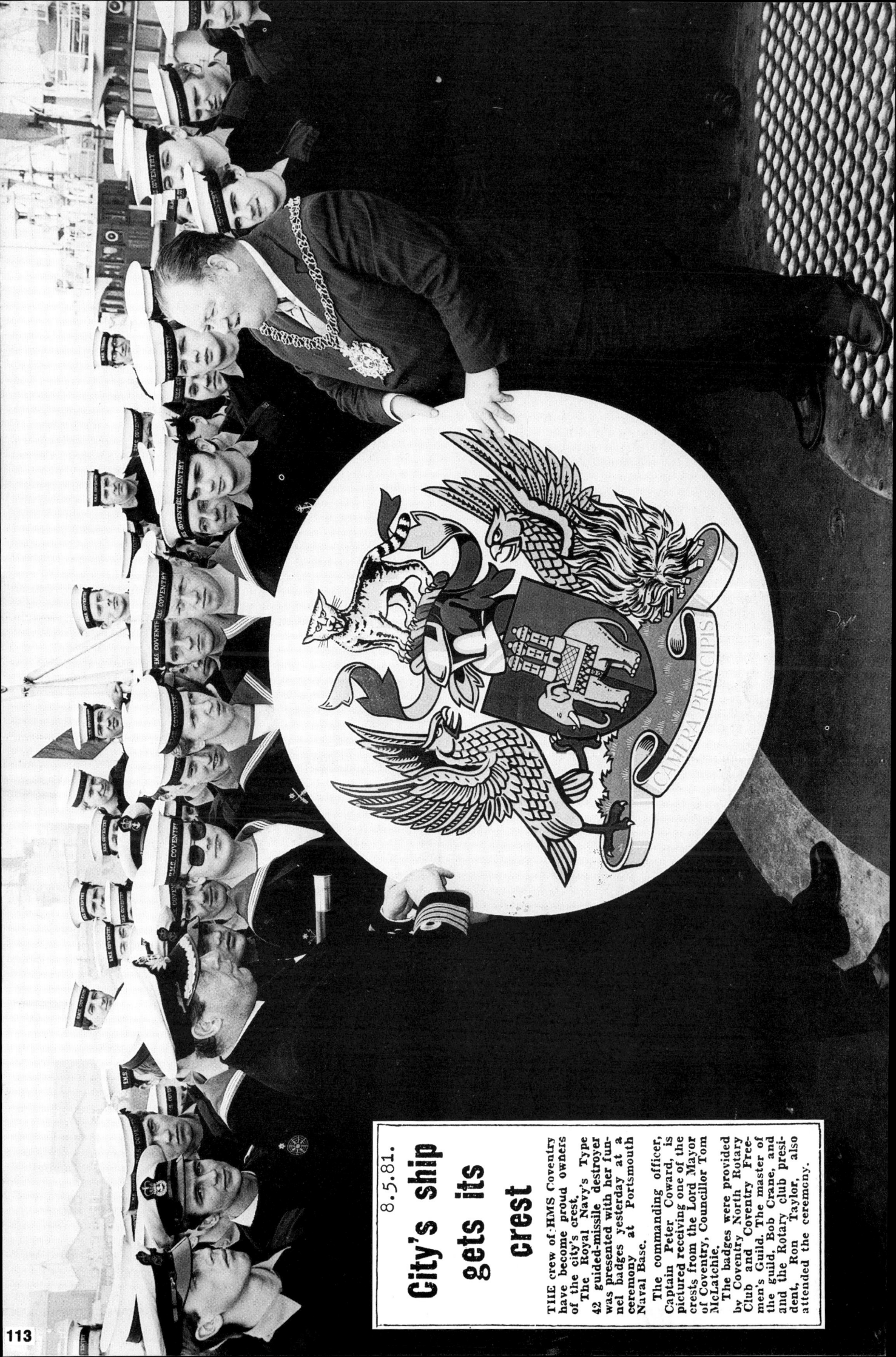

8.5.81.

City's ship gets its crest

THE crew of HMS Coventry have become proud owners of the city's crest.

The Royal Navy's Type 42 guided-missile destroyer was presented with her funnel badges yesterday at a ceremony at Portsmouth Naval Base.

The commanding officer, Captain Peter Coward, is pictured receiving one of the crests from the Lord Mayor of Coventry, Councillor Tom McLatchie.

The badges were provided by Coventry North Rotary Club and Coventry Freemen's Guild. The master of the guild, Bob Crane, and and the Rotary club president, Ron Taylor, also attended the ceremony.

For the love of the Pope . . . over a third of a million people — more than the entire population of Coventry — gathered to greet the Holy Father.

Message that captured the feelings of the faithful

For the love of the people . . . the Pope raises his arms in welcome to the crowd.

AMONG the thousands of flags and banners was one with the simple message: "Thank You."

It captured with two words the feeling when, at 3.15 p.m., a cloud of dust swirled over the crowds and the Pope, who had been theirs was gone.

His helicopter lingered awhile, as if he were reluctant to leave the 350,000 faithful who had waited so long to see him. But after a few minutes it was just an outline against the afternoon sky.

The same gold and blue aircraft's tortuously slow approach that morning had signalled the start of a tumultuous day of contrasting emotions.

It began just after ten o'clock with a burst of noise and colour as John Paul's Popemobile left the helicopter pad to wend through the throngs of pilgrims.

Cheered

This was their moment and it showed on every face. Each would have the memory that for an instant, however brief, the Pope had been theirs alone.

The children and young people screamed and cheered. If they had no banners they waved their arms in a semaphore signal he could not mistake.

And then he was lost to them again, engulfed in a field of golden flags.

Nuns stood on chairs to get a better view of their Holy Father as the band struck up "He's Got The Whole World In His Hands."

John Paul was emotional, too, holding his arms out wide as if embracing the hundreds near him at every inch of his route.

Once, as he raised his hand, the Papal ring was caught in the dazzling sunlight and flashed a signal of his presence round the vast open-air church.

But with the solemnity of

By JON SMITH

the Mass, the mood changed. The faces in the corrals now were attentive, eager for a message. John Paul was garbed in scarlet robes that the wind whipped round him as he spoke.

He gave his message. In a country at war, he raged against war — determined to speak his mind in the city that knows too well the cost of conflict.

Sacrament

The sprawling congregation applauded his passionate plea for peace — he had carried them with him.

Twice more, the mood changed. Both times, John Paul's pilgrims — now enraptured — sensed the atmosphere and responded.

As the confirmation sacrament for 26 candidates ended, the choir took up the words of Pentecost: Veni Sancte Spiritus — Come, Holy Spirit.

Just below me, as the words echoed round, a young girl

reached behind her, without turning her head, to clasp her mother's hand.

Moments later, that private gesture was repeated by the vast crowd when, as priests moved among them to prepare for Communion, they were invited to take their neighbour's hand as a sign of peace.

They did . . . reaching out in 350,000 friendships.

The Communion priests moved out along the aisles under the shade of thousands of gold and white umbrellas. They went to every group of people, forging out from the Papal sanctuary to make the pattern of the spokes of a giant wheel, with John Paul at its hub.

With this gesture the Pope and his pilgrims were bound together.

At the end of the service he moved across the dais, arms outstretched once more, beckoning the congregation

towards him, smiling to the groups of children close by him on his left.

They raced to the fence nearest him, the way they knew he must take to leave the altar platform. Nuns hurried after them, eager too.

The carnival returned as John Paul took lunch. A group of children danced in the early afternoon heat wearing helmets donated by policemen on guard duty. They even paused for one of the officers to take a snapshot.

Dust cloud

But the joy did not last. After his meal, the Pope did not step on to the dais again. His Popemobile took him straight to a waiting helicopter.

To the same furious flag waving that had greeted him earlier, he departed.

The dust cloud thrown up by the whirring rotor blades drifted away. So did the people.

And somewhere somebody is folding up a banner that said simply: "Thank You."

350,000 friends . . . linked hand in hand

THE PAPAL VISIT TO ENGLAND AND WALES
Province of Birmingham

POPE JOHN PAUL II BRITISH VISIT 1982

FEAST OF PENTECOST
Coventry Airport
Sunday 30 May 1982

WHAT a cracker! This is the Christmas present that Jaguar workers promised themselves.

And it came — bang on time, 36 hours before Santa sets off on his annual delivery round.

The gleaming, gold coloured XJ6 which drove off the Brown's Lane assembly line yesterday afternoon to a roof-lifting cheer was the 22,000th Jag built this year.

"What a superb Christmas present," said manufacturing director Mike Beesley. "Everyone has worked so hard this year.

23.12.82

Prince Michael of Kent tours the Talbot car factories with plant director Colin Hudson, Ryton, May 17, 1983

116

Moseley Junior School 50th anniversary celebrations, June 8, 1983

The Lord Mayor of Coventry, Coun. Walter Brandish, names the city's Air Museum bomber, as the last flying Vulcan jet bomber makes the final fly-past, August 30, 1984

Coventry Evening Telegraph, Tuesday, June 15, 1982

Coventry Evening Telegraph

Founded by W. I. Iliffe
February 9, 1891

Falklands next step

THE Falkland Islands victory is a magnificent achievement for British forces, even though the cost in killed and wounded was higher than those of us back home had feared.

And it is because of the commitment which went into restoring freedom to a handful of islanders that the future of the Falklands will not be easy to resolve.

Patently it is unthinkable that Argentina should have any influence. That country's chances of doing so — and at one time they were considerable — were thrown away with the invasion.

It is equally impossible for the Falklands to continue as in the past — neglected and virtually unwanted. The attitude of successive governments (and Parliament) was reflected in the pigeon-holing of the 1976 Shackleton Report on the future of the islands with barely a murmur of protest.

Now the islands have to be viewed differently. We have declared in the strongest possible terms our stake in them. That will mean securing them either by a permanent British garrison or by international protection.

Anne Diamond, Derek Jameson and Tony Blackburn help to launch Coventry Cable television, September 13, 1985

Jaguar, March 28, 1985. Leather-cutter Ted Cross shows the Queen Mother the original 1941 photograph, taken when they first met at Coventry & Warwickshire Hospital. Ted was then part of the Royal Guard of Honour

Princess Alexandra and her husband, the Hon. Angus Ogilvy (later Sir), visit the Royal Show, July 3, 1985

The Princess of Wales visits Remploy, October 16, 1985

A trip on Concorde is the prize in a poster competition organised by The Coventry and Warwickshire Industry Year Group for talented youngsters, July 1, 1986

The Grapevine Bistro, Hay Lane, September 25, 1986

THE triumphant heroes come home.

And for the city of Coventry it's a magical and quite unforgettable day.

Paper flutters from windows and vast crowds cheer as the bus carrying the victorious Sky Blues makes its way through the city centre.

Standstill

Crowds 20-deep lined the streets. Cheering fans stretched along Walsgrave Road, the ring road came to a standstill and city centre streets turned sky blue in a heaving mass of emotion.

The scene was the same along the entire six-mile route of yesterday's cavalcade to welcome home the FA Cup winners.

COVENTRY CITY F.C.
F.A. CUP WINNERS
F.A. YOUTH CUP WINNERS
1987 1987

TRANSPORT MUSEUM
· COVENTRY ·

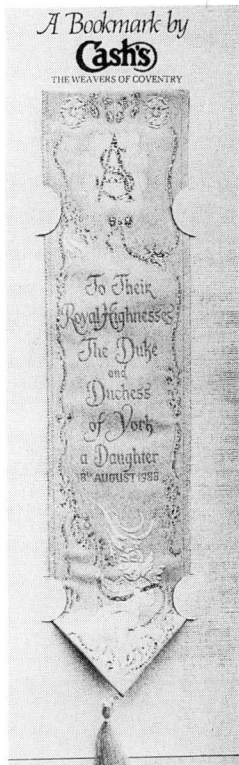

The Duchess of York unveils a plaque to commemorate the opening of the new intensive care unit at the Walsgrave Hospital, October 15, 1987

Coventry Airport, May 27, 1988

Managers from nine expanding firms mark the opening of a new industrial centre in Parbrook Close, Tile Hill South, November 15, 1988

The Princess Roy arrives to open th Polytechnic's ne occupational thera school, May 11, 198

Prince Charles jokes with pub landlord Colum Nugent when he arrives to open a new training centre in St Columba's Close, September 5, 1989

THE main entrance to Coventry Council House will be rebuilt at a cost of £134,000.

Councillors have approved a scheme to install automatic doors, a ramp to allow access for disabled people, new steps and landscaping

The existing revolving door, which is dangerous and prevents wheelchair access, will be removed.

Alternative

A podium, with steps and pillars, will be built outside the entrance with a gently sloping ramp to allow wheelchair access. Flower tubs and decorative lighting are also planned.

The entrance will be closed for around four months while the work takes place.

1.8.89

STARLEY ROAD

A shining example of community spirit. Residents mark a final chapter in their successful bid to save their road from demolition, June 19, 1990

The Duke of Gloucester (left) shares a joke at the Royal Show with the Chairman and Managing Director of Coventry Newspapers Ltd, Frank Bunting, July 5, 1990

Drink to a new bylaw

THERE can be no doubt that the experimental bylaw banning on-street drinking in the heart of Coventry has been a great success.

The city centre is now a more pleasant and safer place, free from the beer-swilling gangs rampaging around in a yobbish and threatening manner.

No wonder other cities want to copy Coventry's example.

The only unfortunate aspect of the new law is it's catch-all nature. In clamping down on the hooligans and the winos it also restricts responsible drinkers.

Owners of licensed premises like Brown's cafe bar in the Lower Precinct and the Belgrade Theatre would like to allow customers to enjoy a meal and a drink outside on the pavement — but the bylaw has prevented this.

Other pavement bars and bistros would add some life and gaiety to the city centre.

It ought to be possible to defeat the yob without placing such draconian restrictions on the enjoyment of the vast majority of law-abiding citizens.

Let the bylaw be redrafted to loosen the net around those it was not meant to catch.

21.12.89.

A MARATHON phone-in on the Mercia Sound airwaves crashed the Snowball appeal past £100,000 yesterday.

The Mercia Sound Goldrush, 18 hours of fund-raising on the air, raised a fantastic £24,000 by midnight last night, with money still coming in.

All day, pledges of money flooded into the Hertford Place studio to show just how much the local people care about the sick and disabled children of Coventry and Warwickshire.

People phoned in bids for interesting and unusual items, most of which money normally could not buy.

A FEW
LOCAL
PERSONALITIES

n Siddeley, managing director of the famous car company, with one of the first cars he designed, 1934

Brian Matthew, BBC announcer, 1958. He went on to become an extremely popular presenter of radio music

Dixon, not only a great comedian but also one of the greatest pantomime dames, 1954

Frank Ifield, 1967, whose record "I Remember You" was a major hit, went on to become a highly successful Country & Western singer

David and Pauline Conway, 1969. David is a Coventrian and in 1960 appeared as one of the Three Monarchs in the Spring Show. This popular husband and wife act completed a world cruise in 1990 entertaining musically, as always, in their own inimitable way

Philip Larkin, poet, writer and jazz reviewer, 1972

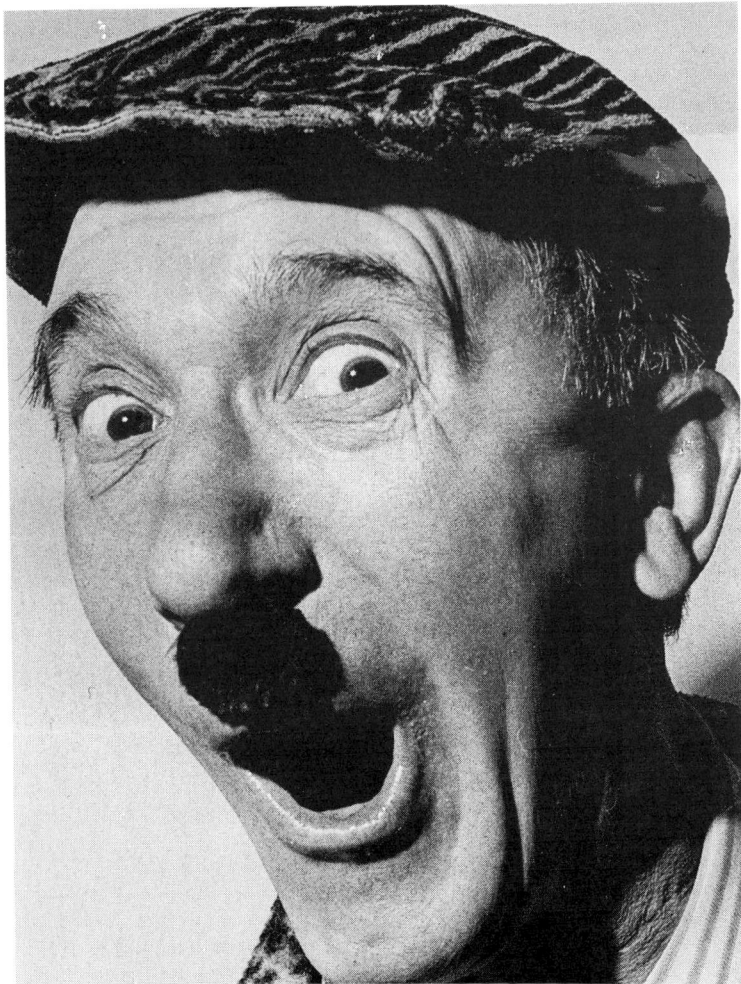

Nat Jackley, "the rubber-necked comedian", one of the funniest visual performers of all time, moved to the city in 1975. In the early days of the war he appeared in Coventry in the show "Roll Out the Barrel", which was a great success, raising enough money to buy a Spitfire. His last of many appearances in the city was in 1983 with Ken Dodd in "Aladdin"

Billie Whitelaw, notable actress of stage, TV and films, 19...

ger Vince Hill had several hit recordings, including "Edelweiss." Here he relaxes at home with his family, 1986

Richard Keys, TV-AM presenter, 1986

Sir Frank and Lady Whittle, seen at the unveiling of a bust of Sir Frank in Church Street, June 15, 1987. Fifty years earlier he had invented the jet engine

129

Dave Willetts, 1989, seen with Petula Clark in the musical "Someone Like You", also starred in "The Phantom of the Opera"

Denzil Pugh, television and radio actor, 1991. Also Justice of the Peace.

Actor, Clive Owen (right) starred with Leslie Philips in Central TV's drama series "Chancer," 1990

ACKNOWLEDGEMENTS

(For providing photographs, for encouragement and numerous other favours)

Neil Allen; George Bartram Enterprises: Colin Beale; Birmingham Post and Mail Ltd.; Nell Blackburn; Jim Boulton; Frank Bunting; Dave Carpenter; Roger Clinkscales; David and Pauline Conway; Ray Cook; Coventry Evening Telegraph; Coventry Local Studies Library; Beryl and Ted Cross; Nancy Cross; Janet Dance; Clive Hardy; Robert Holmes; Frank Ifield; Pamela Jackley; Pat and John Jenks; Anne Jennings; Lord Mayor's Parlour; Dave Mitty; Janet Narasimham; Terrence O'Neil; Peugeot-Talbot Motor Co. Ltd.; Victor Price; Pat and Denzil Pugh; Gil Robottom; Rolls-Royce Heritage Trust; Ron Rowbottom; Royal Regt. of Fusiliers, St John's House, Warwick; Nora Taylor; June Torode; Edna and Raymond Viner; Rosemary Wilkes; Women's Institute, Keresley and Coundon.

Please forgive any possible omissions. Every effort has been made to include all organisations and individuals involved.

ALTON'S BOOKS — SO FAR!

"Coventry: A Century of News"
"Memories of Birmingham"
"Birmingham Remembered"
"Birmingham at War Vol. 1"
"Birmingham at War Vol. 2"
"Memories of West Bromwich"
"Memories of Dudley"
"Memories of Walsall"
"Memories of the Black Country"
"The Black Country at War"
"Memories of Wolverhampton"
"Memories of Shrewsbury"
"Joe Russell's Smethwick"
"Alton Douglas's Know Your Place"
"Alton Douglas's Celebrity Recipes"

Available at leading booksellers

or

For ORDER FORM please write to:

Alton Douglas,
c/o Circulation Dept.,
Coventry Evening Telegraph,
Corporation Street,
Coventry CV1 1FP